EVOLUTIONARIES

TRANSFORMATIONAL LEADERSHIP:
Missing Link in Your Organizational Chart

A NEW BOOK FROM DR. RANDY HARRINGTON & CARMEN E. VOILLEQUÉ

Dear friend,

Thank you for reading our book. We welcome your feedback and hope to talk with you soon. If you like the book and want to help support us, here are a few things you can do:

- Write a book review for us on Amazon.com! Reviews make a big difference!

- "Like" us on Facebook at the Evolutionaries page.
- Follow us on Twitter @be_evolutionary.
- Write your comments on our weekly blog postings at www.be-evolutionary.com.
- Nominate an Evolutionary leader you know at www.be-evolutionary.com or on Facebook.
- Ask us a question at "Ask the Authors" at www.be-evolutionary.com and we will respond in our monthly audio podcast discussions.

We thank you in advance for your help!

Be Evolutionary!

Randy & Carmen

EVOLUTIONARIES

TRANSFORMATIONAL LEADERSHIP
The Missing Link in Your Organizational Chart

RANDY HARRINGTON, PhD, AND CARMEN E. VOILLEQUÉ

PORTLAND • OREGON
INKWATERPRESS.COM

Front Cover @ Troy Stange / Portland Design Lab, LLC
Cover layout and interior design by Masha Shubin

Publisher: Inkwater Press | www.inkwaterpress.com

Library of Congress Control Number: 2011934228

Paperback
ISBN-13 978-1-59299-636-0 | ISBN-10 1-59299-636-1

Kindle
ISBN-13 978-1-59299-637-7 | ISBN-10 1-59299-637-X

ePub
ISBN-13 978-1-59299-638-4 | ISBN-10 1-59299-638-8

Printed in the U.S.A.
All paper is acid free and meets all ANSI standards for archival quality paper.

1 3 5 7 9 10 8 6 4 2

Table of Contents

Acknowledgments v

Chapter 1: Evolutionaries 1

Chapter 2: Evolutionary Planning................................23

Chapter 3: Evolutionary Leadership 41

Chapter 4: Evolutionary Communication...................51

Chapter 5: Evolutionary Teams.....................................75

Chapter 6: Evolutionary Innovation 88

Chapter 7: Evolutionary Guidance...............................98

Chapter 8: Evolutionary Women 107

Chapter 9: The Code of an Evolutionary..................118

Chapter 10: When Evolutionaries Fail......................124

Conclusion 131

About the Authors 133

Acknowledgments

The first person that we want to thank in the writing of this book is you. The fact that you are taking your valuable time to learn new ideas and to be in dialogue with us is a gift. We have thought about you a lot – the hardships, wins, and big dreams that drive you and make you who you are. And we have huge faith in you and what you can accomplish in the world.

And, of course, this book could never have been written without the people who engaged in conversations with us over the last year to provide much of the key wisdom provided in this book: Captain Steve Ahlberg, Chandra Brown, Todd Davidson, Mike Foley, Geoff Gilmore, Cindy Tortorici, and Scott West. They have our highest gratitude!

We thank our clients for teaching us. We have noticed that when we provide the best value to our clients we tend to also learn the most. It has been an honor (and often an adventure) to see the heroic efforts taken in organizations that are fundamentally transforming who they are and what is possible in the world.

We would also like to thank our colleagues Jackson Hataway and JoAnn Edwards for the good wisdom, consistent support, and for always believing in us.

As we wrote this book, we found ourselves returning again and again to share incredible Evolutionary stories and examples provided by the life and work of one friend in particular. While she is not showcased in this book (she needs a whole book dedicated to her alone!) she lives the Evolutionary life better than anyone we know, and continues to be our constant source for inspiration. If we did not have Chief Judge Ann Aiken of the U.S. District Court, District of Oregon, in our lives, this book may never have been written. Thanks, Ann.

And a special thank you for our families, Patty, Cara, Dana and Gwen Harrington; JP and Claire Voillequé; and all of the other people that put up with us.

WARNING:

The act of reading this book is not neutral. By calling attention to this very special group of people you are now a party to their successes and failures. Evolutionaries are everywhere and they are trying to change the world all the time. Once you begin seeing them, you lose your innocence. You are in the game! We hope you are ready.

EVOLUTIONARIES

Transformational Leaders: The Missing Link in Your Organizational Chart

CHAPTER 1

Evolutionaries

It is extremely difficult to manifest and sustain strategic clarity in a world where thousands of tasks bog down the days and the rules seem to change the moment we gain momentum. The sad truth is that most organizations are simply trying to reduce the frustration of a beleaguered staff who see winning as surviving, biding time until some external force defines their options and direction for good or ill.

Often it is in times such as these that organizational leaders call us. They know things need to change, and they know they need help, but what they often don't know is what kind of help they are looking for. So, they ask us to come in and "do some training" or "facilitate some planning sessions." But what they are really looking for is a kind of positive organizational transformation. More training is not the solution. And they know it isn't the solution, but there isn't another way to talk about transformative change. We lack a common language to define this sort of transformational organizational need. In this book, we will provide a new way to talk about organizational transformation and through these conversations we believe you can achieve the evolution you are seeking for your team, company, or community.

We offer the term *Evolutionaries* to describe the kind of people that lead organizations through transformative change. We believe these leaders MUST be present within the organization itself – they cannot be outside consultants, advisors or coaches. (Of course, as we are actually consultants ourselves, we still believe that outside facilitators provide a crucial role in organizational transformation – just not as *Evolutionaries*.)

An **Evolutionary** is:
- **A Planner:** Evolutionaries need a cause and a good, flexible plan – they need to be attached to a strategic outcome that they are invested in and believe in.
- **A Leader:** Evolutionaries must know the business at hand and possess the kind of "street credibility" with your organization's people that garners trust, respect and followers.
- **A Communicator:** Evolutionaries are experts at delivering clear and inspiring messages. They can adapt to the language culture of those they lead, and they are willing to learn new "languages" as necessary to facilitate positive transformation for an organization.
- **A Teammate:** Evolutionaries aren't just great leaders, they are great teammates and great followers. In fact, if you don't have a strong desire to be a part of a team, or follow great leadership when you see it, you are probably not an Evolutionary.
- **An Innovator:** Evolutionaries are skilled in the business of predicting the future. They know how to identify trends, seek out thought leadership, and be awake and aware of new opportunities; they are open to change, comfortable with ambiguity and highly adaptable.
- **A Guide:** Evolutionaries are masters in the art and science of Guidance. They are confident in the "trail"; they know how to facilitate, inspire, foster trust, stay the course and bring people successfully toward a desired end state.

You need Evolutionaries to help you lead your organization in times of transition. They are the secret weapons of organizations that transform quickly, that are able to adapt and innovate, and rise to any challenge, no matter how unexpected. But make no mistake – Evolutionaries are not superheroes; they are not invincible. Nor are they the only type of leader your organization needs. Evolutionaries are not the best people to lead in times of stability and maintenance. Evolutionaries have weakness: lack of patience, lack of consistency and issues with long-term commitment to name a few." But if it is time for a change in your organization, a transformation, or just a new idea, then you are in need of a good Evolutionary.

Evolutionaries are often given titles like "Turnaround Specialist," "Chief Strategy Officer," "Inventor," or even "Visionary." But Evolutionaries are more than just specialists in change – they are committed to a certain type of change. We believe that Evolutionaries are at heart somewhat idealistic. They have made a commitment to making the future a better place through the change or transformation that they lead. They seek to master the change experience so that they can better guide others toward a higher, altruistic and motivational goal. This sensibility transfers into how Evolutionaries approach their own careers, and how they think about organizational strategy, planning and execution.

We also want to be clear about what Evolutionaries are not. They are not just experts, or smart people, or charismatic leaders. They possess the skills and competencies required to lead transformational change, from the idea to building the right team, to participating in that team to achieve results. Not everyone should want to be an Evolutionary, any more than everyone should want to be a star surgeon. In fact, we might not want an Evolutionary surgeon to operate on us!

Over the last 15 years in our work as consultants in the areas of strategy, change management and organizational development, we have had the opportunity to meet a few memorable Evolutionaries.

This book is really about telling their stories. In the following chapters you will meet some of the best modern Evolutionary leaders we know and you will have the opportunity to learn from their wisdom, experience and advice. For each key area of the Evolutionary personality, our experts will chime in, and we offer our analysis from over a decade of experience working with these remarkable people to change the world!

Evolutionaries

Captain Steve Ahlberg: Captain Ahlberg entered active duty upon receiving a commission in 1972 and in June 1976 was assigned to SEAL Team ONE. Captain Ahlberg's personal decorations include the Legion of Merit (2), Bronze Star, Meritorious Service Medal (2), Navy Commendation Medal (2), as well as numerous other awards and decorations. In addition to his leadership of Navy SEALS teams on three continents during his career, Captain Ahlberg also earned an MBA and a Master of Science Degree in Strategic Intelligence.

Chandra Brown: Ms. Brown has worked for Oregon Iron Works, Inc. (OIW) for over 15 years and has held a variety of positions during her tenure with the company. She is currently President of a newly created subsidiary of OIW called United Streetcar, dedicated to offering American-built streetcars throughout the United States. In 2005, she was selected as one of *Oregon Business Magazine*'s Top 50 Business Leaders in the State. She also serves on many non-profit boards. Ms. Brown has an MBA with an emphasis in international business and marketing from Miami University.

Todd Davidson: Todd Davidson is the CEO of the Oregon Tourism Commission. During his tenure with Travel Oregon, tourism in Oregon has become a $7.7 billion industry in Oregon, employing nearly 88,000 Oregonians. Davidson is a member of numerous boards and commissions including the Travel Industry Association of America, the National Council of State Tourism Directors (NCSTD) and the Western States Tourism Policy Council (WSTPC). He is currently a member of TIA's Executive Committee and was recently elected Chair of the National Council of State Tourism Directors. In August 2006 he was named the State Tourism Director of the Year by the Travel Industry Association (TIA), a non-profit organization representing the U.S. travel industry. Todd received the 1992 Governor's Tourism award from Governor Barbara Roberts for his leadership in Oregon's tourism industry.

Mike Foley: Michael Foley, PhD, is the executive director of the Bluetooth Special Interest Group (SIG). Dr. Foley joined the Bluetooth SIG in mid 2004, with just under one million *Bluetooth*-enabled products shipping per week and around 2,500 member companies. Today, under Dr. Foley's direction, *Bluetooth*-enabled products are shipping at a rate of five million per *day* and membership has swelled to over 15,000 companies. Dr. Foley has pushed through an ambitious roadmap, demanding substantial improvements in interoperability, security, and power consumption. Most recently, Dr. Foley has led the adoption of *Bluetooth* v4.0 – a new version of the Bluetooth specification that will allow for billions of button cell battery powered devices to connect via *Bluetooth* wireless technology. Dr. Foley has been recognized by numerous industry publications for his leadership role at the Bluetooth SIG, including *WirelessWeek*, *EE Times* and *RCR Wireless* and is often called on to speak at key industry events, such as CES, Wireless and Mobile Expo and CTIA. Dr. Foley holds a PhD in Electrical Engineering from Arizona State University.

Geoff Gilmore: Geoff Gilmore, PhD, is the CEO & President of Climax Portable Machine Tools. Dr. Gilmore works with leadership teams to facilitate new learning and its rapid application in order to create record-breaking year-after-year improvements. His goal is to help companies and people set extraordinary visions tied to their passion so that all employees are engaging their hearts and minds to deliver extraordinary year-after-year break-through results. He also works as a corporate champion in building new community systems that dramatically improve the lives of people around the world. Geoff holds B.S. degrees in Chemical Engineering and Metallurgical Engineering from the University of Idaho and a Masters in Business Administration from the University of Portland. He earned his Doctoral degree in Quality and Productivity Management from Portland State University, where he studied while being advised by Dr. W. Edwards Deming. Geoff is also a Registered Professional Engineer and a past American Society for Quality (A.S.Q.) Certified Quality Engineer.

Cindy Tortorici: Cindy Tortorici is the CEO and founder of The Link for Women based in Portland, Oregon. Before founding The Link, LLC, she spent 25 years as a business strategist and executive for Nike Inc, Saks Fifth Avenue and May Company. She is the creator of *A Seat at the Table*, a program that coaches women leaders to engage with courage by using their core strengths. Cindy's most recent civic contributions include serving as a trustee of Girls Inc. of NW Oregon from 2004 to 2008. She is a member of the World Affairs Council of Oregon and was named "One of the 100 Most Powerful Women in Town" by the *NW Women's Journal* in 2007. Cindy received a BS from the University of Wisconsin, Madison, and studied business strategy at Stanford University and through the Wharton School of Business. Cindy is a published author and speaker.

 Scott West: Scott West is currently Chief Strategy Officer at Travel Oregon, the office of the Oregon Tourism Commission. After he earned a finance degree from the University of Oregon, Scott's career followed a path rooted in the tourism and hospitality industry. His executive management experience at Oregon's largest myrtlewood factory and gift shop operation, and at a Native American–owned cultural tourism–based company in Alaska, led Scott into public affairs at the Oregon Lodging Association, where he rose to president and CEO. Instrumental in achieving passage of the landmark Oregon Tourism Investment Proposal, Scott's efforts with both legislators and industry members gained a reliable revenue stream for Travel Oregon, the state's official destination marketing agency.

Special Note:
The chapters in this book are independent. While we think they all offer unique lessons, we don't expect you to read them in order. We encourage you to read those most relevant to your needs first, and then explore the others. To help you identify which chapters might benefit you the most, we offer the following assessments designed to diagnose your Evolutionary needs and potential.

Quiz 1: Do You Need an Evolutionary?

Check the boxes YES or NO

QUESTION	YES	NO
1. Do you struggle to see a clear path for growth in your business over the next 5–10 years?		
2. Are you struggling with silos in your organization?		
3. Do you feel there should be more cross-functional collaboration in your organization?		
4. Do you feel like there is too much waste in your organization (funds, resources, time)?		
5. Do people in your organization lack focus or find it hard to define a common vision?		
6. Do you feel like you are reacting to changes in technology instead of being proactive?		
7. Do you wonder what you should be thinking about for future planning?		
8. Are there areas of expertise that you need in your organization, but struggle to synthesize all of the necessary information?		
9. Is it a chore to go to work each day? Do you feel like you are losing steam in your work?		
10. Do you struggle with finding enough professional challenge in your work? Are you bored?		

If you answered "yes" to five or more of the questions above, it is likely that your organization would benefit from a stronger internal Evolutionary presence. In the chapters that follow, we describe how different types of Evolutionaries can serve an organization in times that require significant transformational change. Read on to find out which sort of Evolutionaries your organization needs, how to identify and recruit them, and how to optimize their potential to meet your strategic goals.

Quiz 2: Are You an Evolutionary?

For the following statements, assign a numerical value (1–5) based on your level of agreement with the statement. Use the scoring structure provided below.

5 – strongly agree   4 – agree   3 – neutral   2 – disagree   1 – strongly disagree

CHANGE

QUESTION	SCORE
Change is a necessity for organizational growth.	
I often feel like the pace of change in my organization is way too slow.	
I often feel like the pace of change in my organization is way too fast.	
Everything can be improved.	
I like the idea of working on entirely new systems, projects and ideas – things that are unproven.	
I can't help myself from solving problems – even if they are not directly related to my world.	
I frequently work without regard to the clock or "normal" workday rhythms.	

Score: _____/35

PLANNING

QUESTION	SCORE
I have a reasonably clear sense of what I intend to accomplish in my professional work over the next five years.	
I approach work from a project perspective; planning, executing, completing, and evaluating all along the way.	
I believe planning is critical for success.	
I think it is reasonable to make 20-year strategic plans.	
I believe too much time is spent on planning.	
With so much uncertainty in the world, long-term planning is basically worthless.	
Once I know the strategic outcome, I am easily able to generate plans to meet the goal.	
When I have a good plan, I am more invested in the mission ahead.	
I don't mind focusing on details, if they lead to a better plan.	

Score: _____ /45

LEADERSHIP

QUESTION	SCORE
I feel comfortable in leadership positions.	
I seek opportunities to lead projects.	
When a new project opportunity arises, I volunteer to lead the project.	
Leadership begins with a vision of what is necessary to achieve specific goals.	

Leadership is a natural trait; some people have it and some don't.	
I am very clear about what is important and what is less important in my day-to-day work.	
I know my industry; I have deep experience.	
I know my industry; I have formal training and/or credentials.	
My peers often seek me out for business/professional advice.	
I motivate the people I work with to obtain organizational goals.	

Score: _____/50

COMMUNICATION

QUESTION	SCORE
I like to give speeches and presentations.	
I like to lead meetings.	
People tell me I am a good writer.	
I read more than one book at a time.	
I am a student of the world – ready and able to learn from other traditions and cultures.	
I can tell a good story.	
I can coach other people to improve their communication skills.	
People often come to me for advice on communication issues.	
I enjoy learning new business "languages" and can adapt quickly to new business environments.	

I am able to speak "across the organization" and make connections between departments.	
I proofread my work carefully.	
I believe in the value of practice, rehearsal, and preparation.	

Score: _____/60

TEAMWORK

QUESTION	SCORE
I value working with others in a team environment.	
Team bonds go beyond the work at hand; teams should be special.	
Real teams can accomplish more than simple groups of people.	
I enjoy competition…and I am competitive.	
Team concepts are overused in the modern corporate environment – they can bog things down.	
Being on a team means checking your ego and being a good follower as well as a good leader.	

Score: _____/30

INNOVATION

QUESTION	SCORE
I read about all kinds of things that are not directly related to my job.	
I am a natural networker; when I meet people I almost always make connections.	
I read more than five professional magazines or journals every month.	

I spend hours each week working to identify future trends that will affect my organization.	
I intentionally network with people outside my professional circle to better understand best practices from other industries and other points of view.	
I am proud of my accomplishments so far, but I know have much more I can do.	

Score: _____/30

GUIDANCE

QUESTION	SCORE
I like to help people learn.	
People say I am a good coach/mentor.	
The people I have taught or coached are often promoted and/or recognized for their work.	
I am able to explain complicated ideas in relatively simple and clear language.	
I believe that teaching is one of the most important forms of influence.	
I am a talented facilitator.	
I am able to listen carefully and facilitate group decision-making.	
I am comfortable working with large groups of professionals representing a diversity of professional points of view.	

Score: _____/40

MORAL CODE

QUESTION	SCORE
I adhere to a clear set of moral and ethical standards.	
I believe I have a responsibility to make the world a better place.	
I am happy to work on efforts that may not come to fruition for several generations.	
I spend active time supporting efforts to help the next generation learn, grow, and be healthy.	
I believe there are fundamental values that are universal.	
I don't think about "retiring"; at some level I always see myself contributing.	
I am driven by inspiration more than a paycheck.	
Business is not just about profit and loss; it is also the place to work on issues like social justice.	
I actively remove myself from people or situations that don't support my core values.	

Score: _____/45

Change Total:	_____/35
Planning Total:	_____/45
Leadership Total:	_____/50
Communication Total:	_____/60
Teamwork Total:	_____/30
Innovation Total:	_____/30
Guidance Total:	_____/40
Moral Code Total:	_____/45
Evolutionary Degrees Total (Grand Total):	_____/335

It may be that you are one of the Evolutionaries that can help to lead your organization forward. Or, it may be that you are interested in increasing your skills by developing your Evolutionary potential. The good news is that Evolutionaries are rarely, if ever, born. These skills can be learned, and are honed over time through conscious attention and application. The quiz you just took will tell you where you fall on what we call the "Evolutionary Development Scale." It will also tell you which areas you are strong and which areas you are weak in your Evolutionary skill set (for example, you may be very strong in Evolutionary Communication skills, but need work in Evolutionary Planning skills). Once you have calculated your score, read the descriptions below to learn where you fall on the Evolutionary Development Scale, and areas you can focus on for improvement.

Evolutionary Degrees:
- Beginner (scores from 65 to 200)
- Apprentice (scores from 201 to 270)
- Guilded (scores from 271 to 325)
- Master (scores from 325 to 335)

It takes time to become an Evolutionary. There are degrees of development. Your quiz score shows you what degree you have already achieved, and now we encourage you to read on for coaching tips you can use as you continue on your Evolutionary path to the next degree of development.

Degrees of an Evolutionary

Beginner: Because most people are not aware that the Evolutionary path exists, to be a beginner as an Evolutionary is to be a part of a rare group of people. To acknowledge the Evolutionary as a "way to be" is an enormous step all on its own. You see the potential of growth and development in the actions that you take every day. It's not a new course you have to take or seminar you need to attend (though these things can help inform your observations), it is part of your daily life – which is rich with potential for learning and excelling. You are awake to the potential of 24/7 learning and you do not feel daunted by it. You look forward to the changes ahead in your life (especially the challenges), and are eager to learn from them.

Coaching tips:

- Learn how to learn from fiction and popular entertainment. If you watch a movie, think about it from the possibility of transformational change. How might it be used as a conversation starter for your next pitch or conflict at work? Or, consider cutting out a cartoon that made you laugh because it was about the failure to learn or the difficulties of change and post it in your office as a reminder.

- Talk to people and listen to people who have gone through significant change. Ask them what was most helpful? What was least helpful? What was surprising? What would they change about the experience? Begin to see yourself as an anthropologist of the change experience in all sorts of different situations.

- Develop a huge appetite for inquiry. Triple the number of questions you are asking on a regular basis. Learn from the everyday.

Apprentice: To be an apprentice is to formalize your learning through seeking out mentorship and intentionally beginning the quest to develop your Evolutionary skill set. You are identifying and forming formal and informal relationships with teachers of all kinds, both within and outside of your industry. You are reaching beyond your current job duties and seeking knowledge in different areas and how to apply that knowledge in different contexts. You are engaging in a course for "learning how you learn," working to achieve not just depth of experience, but breadth of experience. This can look like volunteering on a project led by someone you admire, learning to play a musical instrument, taking a martial arts class, or even doing community work. The point is that you are taking on these new learning endeavors as an effort to better observe your own development style – what makes you better, and how it works to do so. Knowing this about yourself is a powerful driver in your continued development over the course of your lifetime.

And the same breadth of exposure you apply to seeking out these more formal learning experiences should also apply to the books that you read, your media exposure, the places you travel and the events you attend. Increasing the diversity of people, places, academic literature, media, etc., to which you are exposed allows you not only to discover how you learn, but how you fail, how you persevere, and when necessary, how you redirect your efforts. The more you practice these skills, the more "change-ready," adaptable, confident and self-aware you become. You are increasing your ability to adapt to any situation and any experience and you are learning how to take the change experience in stride, even to anticipate it and look forward to the change.

You also realize that you want to make the world a better place and have thoroughly internalized the importance this mission will have in everything you choose to do from this point forward in your life. You have made a commitment to learning and action that is positive and future-oriented. You are making choices now with a strong *intent*.

Coaching tips:
- Broaden your experience and seek learning opportunities using a three-pronged approach (interpersonal, technical, and experiential). Don't just focus on your technical skills or specific job experience. Look for areas that expand your relationship-building opportunities and self-awareness. Seek out new experiences that challenge you to learn and to fail – that stretch you beyond what is comfortable. It is only in situations of the "unexpected" that we can truly adapt,

and Evolutionaries know they must "surprise" themselves in order to develop.

- Test your assumptions about your ability to influence others. For example, consciously take the time to dress more nicely when you go to work or to a social event and carefully observe what sort of reaction you get. How is it different? Or, take time to prepare with more detail for a work presentation and see what kind of feedback you get. Make observations about intentional small changes you make to see if they increase or decrease your ability to influence stakeholders and achieve your goals. Make note of what you learn about your ability to foster change – no matter how small it may seem.

- Set up mini-goals for increasing your breadth of knowledge and experience. Visit a museum you have never been to in your community. Take a pottery class or learn how to dance. Finally read that *War and Peace* novel you have had on your shelf. Listen to the four-hour version of the opera your friend told you about. Take a digital media course or vow to listen to NPR at least 30 minutes each day. You get the idea…

Guilded: You are Guilded when many of the people who meet you, unprovoked, begin to turn to you, count on you, and assign to you the privileges of thought leadership that come with being an Evolutionary. You are able to legitimately claim the face of a person who is positively future-focused and able to yield results where others would have struggled or failed. You have a history, a track record, of time in your life that demonstrates you have "been there, done that, and succeeded against the odds." You have a legacy of experience, good and bad, that you have the ability to draw on both for professional credibility and for problem solving strategy and technique. ***Note: This does not mean that you have gray hair!*** Some of the Guilded Evolutionaries we know are quite young. This does not mean that they are smarter than those of us that developed later in life, but it does mean they probably had a head start. Some people began their Evolutionary development as children. Perhaps they were raised in a way that offered highly diverse exposure opportunities and lots of change. Maybe you know a young Evolutionary that was lucky enough to experience several different cultures, classes, countries, languages, and educational programs in their youth. Maybe you worked in a field hospital in Darfur for two years in your early twenties. The point is, many people have taken the accelerated course in "change-readiness" through their unique early life experience.

Whether early in life, or later, the key to becoming an Evolutionary is that you have taken higher risks than most, you have failed more often or more deeply than most, and you know how to overcome failure. You have also achieved formal levels of certification in your field and recognition within the various disciplines that you are pursuing or have pursued in the past. You have racked up achievements in life in general, doing things that most other people have not attempted unless they are exceptionally driven. Finally, you have come to the realization that to really do important things in the world you cannot do it alone. You have come to respect the power of the collectivity and know how to harness that power to achieve future-ready goals. And you are compensated, promoted, and professionally rewarded for this special talent.

Coaching tips:
- Learn how to set expectations with other people so that you are not being unfair to them. It is classic for a Guilded Evolutionary to identify a talent in another person and call it out. It is also likely that talented people will present themselves to you because they recognize your Evolutionary quality. But it is perhaps a downfall of the Evolutionary that he or she tends to see the ultimate potential – the peak possibility – in each person that comes along and not tend to the situational realities, personal limitations, and series

of events that may impede the realization of that potential. So, it is important that you don't set false expectations for when and how the Evolutionary work, ideas, innovations and transformation you propose in the team, organization or the world at large will really be done. You need to identify and enlist talented people to assist in your efforts, but be careful not to promise them more than you can deliver. (Evolutionaries have been accused of talking "pie in the sky" more than a time or two!)

- Form unlikely, but successful professional partnerships, even if you are not directly involved with them. Introduce great leaders you know to other top performers. Create synergies between volunteer efforts in your community that you know overlap or share goals. Connect vendors with other companies that might benefit from a partnership. Demonstrate your ability to build connections and bring people and entities together in ways that could never be done without your assistance, even when you and your company are not the beneficiary of the partnerships.

- Seek out long-standing problems that need to be addressed and apply your talent to trying to solve those problems that others find too challenging. Choose these problems carefully – make sure they align with your commitment to building a positive future.

- As an Apprentice Evolutionary your job was to broaden your knowledge and experience. Now, as a Guilded Evolutionary you must begin to narrow your focus. Choose some challenges and problems where you can make a difference in your organization, community and world, and muster the vast resources you have accumulated in your life to tackle the monster issues that you most care about. Figure out the value-driven mission or missions that you will spend the next 10 years of your life working on.

- Be engaged in teaching others. You should spend much

more time in "teaching" mode than in "doing" mode on a daily basis. Embrace your role as mentor, coach, and guide to others.

Master: The big shift toward mastery is that you are no longer doing just one job. You have risen above any job description or position and what you do is now *your life*. There is no differentiation between who you are and the many things that you do. This is not the same thing as being a "workaholic," though it can look similar to outsiders. What it means is that you are always operating in the *Evolutionary state of being*. They say the Dalai Lama is always in a state of meditation, he just chooses to adjust or intensify his state over the course of the day to address the present (what is in front of him at the time). Similarly, you also may hold a job title, but as far as you are concerned, you are on a much bigger journey in your work and your life and beyond than what can be detailed in a standard job description. You are focused on impacting things that go well beyond your company and even beyond your own life span. You are thinking about how to make a positive difference that will be relevant and endure for generations. Almost all your time is now devoted to the teaching and guidance of others in all areas of your work and life. But you are also in a perpetual mode of listening and learning. Everything in life is a teaching and learning moment; all experience is adding to the vast and complex tapestry. You no longer have the experience of fear and intimidation around change. You are comfortable and ready for even the most unexpected of circumstances because you live perpetually in an Evolutionary state of being and trust your responses to that change. You are able to accurately judge the ability of an individual or a team to perform at full capacity. (Note: we are rarely able to do any of this well, let alone maintain this level of achievement consistently, which is why it is often identified as "magic" when people see it in action.)

Coaching tips:
- Be careful of your own ego. Repeat over and over the

mantra, "It's not about me." You are *facilitating* the development of others, you are not developing them. You are facilitating transformational change in the world, but you are not a "change-maker." Be the master of your ego.

- Be very discerning about the projects that you take on. As a master Evolutionary, you will be offered a flood of opportunities because of your strong problem-solving talent. Just like anyone else, you have a fixed amount of time and resources, and even at maximum capacity you are limited. Just because you *can* do something doesn't mean you *should* do it. Be careful where you choose to devote your time.

- Be constantly reinforcing your own humility. People are going to give you a lot of positive feedback and accolades. But if you start to really need that recognition, it is a problem. Take on learning something totally new each year so you remember what it is like to be "dumb," to fail or to just be inept at something. Let those that admire you watch you learn something new – it is humbling for you, and inspirational for them.

- Realize that what you say and do ripples out beyond your sphere of perception; many people will repeat your words, share your wisdom and relay your ideas to others they know. Your reach is much further than that of the average person. So, you have a more heightened responsibility for your words and actions than others might have. You are more in the public eye than most people, and so it is worse when you violate that public trust.

CHAPTER 2

Evolutionary Planning

Evolutionary Wisdom

The following quotes provide insight from interviews with several of our Evolutionaries addressing the topic of strategic planning and approaches to transformative organizational change. We start with Cindy Tortorici, the CEO of the Link for Women, sharing her philosophy for where all great planning needs to begin – with a reason for being.

CINDY TORTORICI: In my work as a strategic planner, I often draw from the concept of the "Golden Circle" created by Simon Sinek. Sinek explains that when you ask people about their organizational strategy, they almost always start with the "What"; they will tell you what the business does. If you push them harder they will go to "How" – how their business gets work done, or how they serve customers, but rarely are people able to tell you their "Why" – why they do the business they do – why it matters. The best leaders tell their story in the opposite direction, starting with Why and moving out to the How and the What. I believe that at its core, leadership is about trust, and trust starts with Why. Especially in this economic environment, people are looking for leaders they can trust. These are the people they will choose to follow.

When you know your organization's reason for being, you can

begin to plan with confidence, even if you don't know all of the answers and the future is unpredictable. Todd Davidson of Travel Oregon explains the need to consider what you can plan for and the role disruption plays in good planning.

TODD DAVIDSON: *I subscribe to the theory that you plan for those things that you can control and you prepare for the things you can't plan for. We knew what the power of the Travel and Tourism industry was because we invested in the research. The research helped confirm a gut instinct we already had. The potential was clear, but we had no funding. I have a Chinese symbol on my office wall that stands for "crisis" and "opportunity" because they are basically two sides of the same character. At Travel Oregon, we were in a situation where crisis met opportunity. And so, we put very methodical thought into what we needed to do. We developed a clear purpose and we began to staff toward that purpose. We recruited the people we needed. We didn't go out and hire a bunch of people all at once – we hired people as the work grew and the consumer demand started to evolve, so we have some of the same positions, but we also changed some positions and created some new positions so that people could flow to the work. And, we approached our strategic plan as the dynamic animal that it is. It has got to be written in a way that recognizes that it is going to change, it's going to evolve so this is not a one-time conversation, this is an ongoing dialogue that we are having with one another. So if you have an idea of what we can do better, higher, faster, stronger, then tell us and we want to see if there is a way to incorporate that and if not we will let you know intelligently and politely and professionally why not.*

Todd's story teaches us that great plans don't just emerge out of good planning conversations alone, they extend into excellent documentation, the facilitation of stakeholder feedback, and intentional organizational development to align with the plan. Scott West works with Todd to drive the planning process at Travel Oregon, and he describes additional challenges to the planning process when considering opportunities and calculated risk:

SCOTT WEST: *There was a clear opportunity for Travel Oregon to innovate and lead in state tourism, but we had been approaching the problem in an institutional manner. In a recession, we weren't getting our traditional revenue sources; we knew taxes weren't going to be raised, so we were left trying to think about how to avoid being served a plate of cold food at the children's table. We had to shift our focus and our planning to local revenue – new ways to think about revenue. Our approach became much more entrepreneurial, creating programs like the Regional Cooperative Marketing Program to instill a sense of organization throughout the state and reinforce all these relationships that had already existed but were untapped.*

Scott touches on the need to leverage partnerships in the new economy that organizations and systems may have taken for granted in the past. This is a dramatic shift in how to think about planning. At our planning firm, Strategic Arts and Sciences, we have a name for this kind of approach to planning: Meta-Planning. We think in the next decade all planning will have to be more inclusive of internal and external partners in the strategic ecosystem.

We believe that to succeed in this new Meta-Planning environment, plans have to be more transparent. Producing the kind of plan that is not only functional, but intended for public consumption, requires a "public-facing" orientation to the planning process from the very beginning. It's not enough to just have a plan that everyone buys into and everyone can execute from, it has to be something you are proud to put in the window for passersby to read. That is a pretty sophisticated piece of work. Producing this sort of plan goes beyond the traditional realm of "strategic planning." And that is exactly what Todd Davidson, Scott West and Travel Oregon decided they needed to do *[see sidebar on page 37 for more on this story of partnerships and planning].*

Evolutionaries know the importance of good planning. But they also know when to move ahead – even when the plan is not perfect. Chandra Brown shares some of her experience and wisdom on how to know when it's time to move from planning to action.

CHANDRA BROWN: *Planning is about more than vision—you have to know when your plan is "good enough" to move ahead. You must be continually moving forward and continually implementing. There is a common saying that really resonates with me: "Vision without implementation is just Hallucination." Here at Oregon Iron Works we know that the engineers can redesign for a thousand days in a row and they will never make a perfect design. It's my role as a leader to tell the engineers when needed, that "We need to find a 90 percent solution and then when we reach 90 percent we are going to break your pencils." It can take a lot to convince people that a plan doesn't have to be perfect. But our success has come from knowing that planning is only as good as how well it allows you to continue to progress. You are not going to be able to wait for the hundred percent solution so the job in my opinion of an excellent leader is to be able to take in the massive amounts of information and data and be able to make a cut at a certain point. In my experience that last 10–20 percent toward perfection takes the greatest amount of time, so in order to keep moving forward I am happy with 80 to 90 percent. Great leaders are those people that will come in and make the decision that this is the time to move on with a not perfect solution but a pretty darn good one.*

Chandra Brown's approach to planning is Evolutionary. It's taking a calculated risk – making a bet (with 80% odds) that an idea is ready for execution. This may be one of the pivotal differences between an Evolutionary Planner and any other type of planner. It's not that Evolutionary Planners are superior, but that their tolerance for risk is fueled by a healthy appetite for innovation and transformative change. They are confident they can adapt to bumps along the way, and they are willing to let progress trump perfection when it comes to making key decisions.

Like Chandra, the Navy SEALs are no strangers to calculated risk. As evidenced by the recent operation to locate and eliminate Osama Bin Laden, there are few organizations in the world, public or private, that can rival the SEALs when it comes to planning. But even the most seasoned Navy SEAL will tell you that plans almost always do not go as planned. The ability to plan in excruciating detail, and then, as Chandra Brown suggests, proceed knowing you will need to be adaptable and make adjustments on the fly is the "secret sauce" of Evolutionary transformation. Maybe that's why the Navy SEALs call their training exercises "Evolutions."

CAPTAIN STEVE AHLBERG: To me, planning was always the worst part of an operation because it was so excruciating. To plan well you have to first clearly define the desired end state and develop a general concept of operations as to how to achieve that desired end state. Detailed planning is then done by breaking the general concept into attainable bite-sized chunks, or phases. Then you break each phase into several steps and "what if" each of those steps and you come up with, say, the three most likely things that could go wrong in each step of each phase and then you "what if" those. It is a painstaking process. You have to plan it to death covering all potential "what ifs" so when you actually go into the field you are confidently ready for anything. You never know which one of those "what ifs" is going to occur but typically one or more of them will. Detailed planning makes you more and more familiar with what it is you are trying to achieve and can result in modifications to the original desired end state. Detailed planning makes you committed to achieving the desired end state successfully, and flexible in dealing with evolving unintended consequences that may occur during the execution phase. Involve the whole team in the planning process so everyone knows the plan well and all the "what ifs" that might happen. You do that so if somebody goes down, if somebody gets hurt, somebody else can fill in because everyone knows the plan. Everyone involved receives the same intelligence. There is no intelligence, for example, that is held only for the platoon commander, it's given to everybody, even the most junior people in the platoon, and that's key. If everyone involved doesn't have all available intelligence the best ideas may be suppressed and, when discovered by the platoon, confidence in the leadership will be shaken. In the Teams sometimes the most junior people will have the best ideas. I have seen in the business world where some of the young people who have only been employed a short time have great ideas but are afraid to speak up and their leadership isn't receptive to even hearing the ideas if they do. As the leader of a real

Team, you need to suppress your ego so you can be open and accepting to the ideas of others, even your most junior people.

Captain Ahlberg cautions that Evolutionary plans are best when everyone that is part of making the plan a reality has some input into the plan – they have a chance to put their "fingerprints" on the process in some meaningful way. Plans are not handed down from on high to the front line to execute. Evolutionary planning recognizes that in order to accomplish transformative change, everyone needs to own the plan from the beginning. This means open dialogue up and down the organization.

Mike Foley of Bluetooth SIG has been championing open dialogue as an integral part of the planning process for years now – but he emphasizes how this works at the Board of Directors level. For Bluetooth SIG, the key to Evolutionary Planning is to be future-focused in planning dialogues. To transform regularly (a must in high-paced technology) you have to already live in the future. His planning sessions are primarily devoted to aspirational vision. And his organization is reaping the benefits.

MIKE FOLEY: *I think planning works the best when we are having open-ended discussions about what the technology should be or what our goals are for three to five years out – when we really give ourselves permission to explore all the possibilities, especially those that seem impossible with today's technology. We definitely think about some short-term goals and how to excel in today's marketplace, but we spend more time looking at the bigger picture and where we want to go in the future. Once I know where we believe we can go, where we want to go, then I can work to put the pieces together to figure out how to get there. Our board reviews short-term plans, but we really focus on the long-term, larger picture and try not to get mired in the day-to-day details. We run smoothly. Anyone can look at the scoreboard and see if you are doing well, but it takes a bit more of an art to decide what belongs on the scoreboard. That is the real value of our board and their expertise and creativity.*

Why You Need an Evolutionary Planner

You will know you have an Evolutionary planner in the room when he or she will continually get off track, into deep water, into other people's "turf," and frustrated in planning conversations that foot to the annual budget. There is nothing wrong with having good old-fashioned tactical budget planning conversations. But an Evolutionary planner will become very uncomfortable if that conversation takes the place of a real strategic/Evolutionary plan for your organization.

The Evolutionary planner knows that a good strategic plan has to offer daily, relevant, and easily understandable guidance for thousands of decision points, communications, and actions that cannot be conceptualized or predicted. Good plans have to be both resolute and flexible.

Evolutionary plans are:
- **Short.** They can be read in a single sitting.
- **Simple.** They are easily understandable to people inside of and outside of the organization.
- **Flexible.** They flip the funnel, allowing for more options at the conclusion of each planning phase instead of forcing choices too early.
- **Public.** They are accessible, value-driven, and something you are proud to share.
- **Inclusive.** Everyone in the organization should see themselves in the plan and be responsible for the plan.
- **Factual.** The plan makes use of a wide range of evidence from external empirical data points to informal media clips of customer needs.
- **Common Sense.** They have a "face validity" to them.
- **Emotional.** They evoke allegiance, excitement, and direct action.
- **Art.** They are professionally, artistically presented.

How Evolutionaries Plan

Evolutionaries accept that plans can change, and they know when to alter a plan to meet the end goal. This often happens in the business world – you plan and as soon as you are done planning, the economic environment changes or new competition moves in and the plan is already obsolete. So, it makes sense to ask: Why even plan? The answer Evolutionaries know is because the way you plan can have a game-changing impact, no matter what may happen in the actual game.

From the wisdom offered by our Evolutionaries in this chapter we learn that the planning process helps drive commitment to the strategy, even if the plan ends up changing later. What's more, planning together as a team also helps drive confidence in responses to those "what if" situations that will inevitably occur.

We learn that planning really has two parts: there's planning and then there's "now we have the plan…" Evolutionaries are not just skilled in framing the plan; they are skilled in selling the plan and executing on the plan. They can Tarzan between these skills easily – whereas most other people can't.

Evolutionary Planners:
- *Commit to the mission*
- *Master the plan*
- *Are comfortable with ambiguity*
- *Display adaptability*

Evolutionary planners are successful planners because they *commit to the mission* at hand. Buying into the desired end state of the plan may seem like a no-brainer for success, but you might be surprised by how many executives do not really commit to or have a deep belief in the goals they say that they are trying to achieve. Cindy Tortorici tells us that we have trouble buying into our plans when we don't really identify with why we are doing the planning in the first place. Evolutionary planners take the time to discover what Ms. Tortorici calls their "Why" for acting, and this allows them to be confident throughout the planning process. *"The best leaders tell their story by starting with Why and moving out to the How and the What. At its core, leadership is about trust, and trust starts with Why."* Evolutionaries can easily communicate why the plan is good because they know where the plan is leading and possess a strong belief in the value of the end result.

Evolutionary planners *master the plan*. They know it forwards and backwards, inside out and upside down. They know every nuance and every alternate scenario, every back-up plan and every team substitution. Todd Davidson and Scott West show us how knowing the plan allowed them to be methodical and unwavering in the execution. Once they made the commitment to transform, deviating from the plan was only an option if the landscape began to shift. Knowing the plan inside out allowed their organization to be dynamic in using the plan to achieve their mission. Mr. Davidson explains the importance of applying "very methodical thought" into what Travel Oregon needed to do by considering everything from how the plan would be written, to how to recruit and hire the right people to execute on the plan. Travel Oregon reorganized to align positions with consumer demands discovered during the planning process, better enabling their people to "flow to the work." By mastering the plan and helping each member of their organization to also master the plan, Todd Davidson and Scott West were able to make extremely difficult decisions for their organization around staffing and structure that might otherwise have shaken the foundations. No one said transformation was easy – but Evolutionaries know that a good plan can prepare people for the disruption that always comes with change.

Evolutionary planners are *comfortable with ambiguity* and are willing to take a certain amount of risk to move a plan forward and maintain momentum. Evolutionaries are change agents in the organization, and in order to change, Evolutionaries know the most important thing is to keep the team moving. Chandra Brown advises us that we cannot wait for the "perfect" plan – Evolutionaries take action once a plan is "good enough." "As a leader it's my job to determine when a project is ready to go from paper to being built – that without strong leadership our incredibly eager and creative engineers who have given 100% on a project would continue to tweak designs without an end in sight. There must be a limit to how many times you can go back to the drawing board because many times you've reached the solution and it's time to implement, keeping the project on time and within schedule." Ms. Brown teaches us that the most successful planners from vision to execution are those that will move forward with some degree of ambiguity in the plan. Evolutionaries bring transformational change to organizations precisely because they push forward when others are uncertain. It's not about abandoning the value of comprehensive planning, it's about knowing when to say the appropriate attention to the plan has been achieved.

Finally, Evolutionaries *display adaptability*. We learn from Captain Ahlberg that often the minute that you move into an operational mode the situation changes and the plan has to be adapted to achieve the desired end state. Captain Ahlberg tells us that the Seal teams plan, plan, plan. And then they plan some more. But let's fast-forward to the plan's completion. We have planned until we puke. We've got it all stuffed in our heads, we have built 3D models, and we've "what if'd" every scenario until the plan is mastered. Then, as Captain Ahlberg explains, five minutes into the operation the situation shows up as being completely different, the wheels come off and it's time to adapt the plan. This is where Evolutionaries become invaluable. They are comfortable with ambiguity, confident in the mission and the team and able to adapt quickly to keep things on track to achieve the desired end state. Evolutionaries are not easily flustered in times of uncertainty, because they anticipate the unexpected and train themselves to respond as a matter of course.

Like Captain Ahlberg, the best Evolutionary leaders bring calm to chaos. Evolutionaries are pros at sharing the planning process and repeating the plan and all of its scenarios over and over until everyone knows it so well it guides team actions unerringly. Ahlberg reminds us that in the Seal teams *"Everyone knows the plan. Everyone has the same intelligence."* Evolutionaries know that everyone on the team will need to display adaptability when the situation inevitably changes, and the best way to help people adapt to new situations is to make sure everyone on the team knows what is expected. Evolutionary planning is not about holding all the cards and heroically doling out ideas when the time is at hand. Evolutionaries make sure the plan belongs to everyone from the very beginning.

Evolutionary Challenge

Meet Roger. As a long-term executive with your senior leadership team, Roger is the deep well of the old ways in your organization. Roger is the guy who will remind you, "We tried to do that very thing in 1984 and it didn't work because…" Roger is also the guy who is currently in charge of the strategic planning meetings that will inform the annual budgeting process. His response to this challenge has been to hold a meeting with the leadership team where he facilitated a SWOT analysis. The results of that analysis were turned into a two-page email sent out to the leadership team and department heads under the title "Guidance for Budgeting." Roger was surprised that there was so much confusion, frustration and misdirection in the budgeting priorities that came back from the various departments. But not all is lost. Roger's analysis called out five areas of urgency for your organization. They are the following:

1. Improving speed and efficiency in core data processing
2. Bringing more relevant data into the marketing cycle
3. Assessing global competitors more effectively
4. Improving service quality in web and retail outlets
5. Improving employee compliance training

Now meet Jan. Jan is an assistant to the Vice-President of Human Resources. Jan listened to her supervisor vent about Roger recently. As she listened, she thought, "The work that Roger's done is good, it's just not complete." Jan saw very clearly the next steps that were necessary to turn Roger's first effort into a successful, clear, measurable strategic plan that would inspire employees. What did Jan see?

Here are a few ideas to get you started:

- The first thing Jan realizes is that there is no single "right" plan that will solve for all the strategic issues facing the organization. She sees the need for more flexibility and adaptation to build into the plan.
- Next, Jan recognizes that single strategic priorities should accomplish multiple objectives. This means that all five challenge areas identified by Roger could be improved with an organization-wide strategic focus on, for example, *quality*.
- Instead of building a strategic plan that tries to engineer solutions for individual problems, Jan see a plan that would call out the fundamental interdependence of every department and person in the company and provide a simple story that motivates people.
- Finally, Jan sees Roger's work as a great resource for identifying performance measures for employees and departments. The challenges in Roger's email all represent dependent variables that should change as the result of a sustained strategic effort.
- Jan realizes that Roger's mistake was to believe that the SWOT analysis yielded independent variables that could be manipulated for strategic ends. In other words, Roger had it backwards.

Brainstorm your ideas in the space below:

_____

_____

_____

_____

_____

_____

_____

_____

_____

_____

_____

_____

_____

_____

_____

What advice would you give Jan for sharing and executing on these ideas?

_____

_____

_____

_____

_____

_____

_____

_____

_____

_____

_____

_____

In summary, Evolutionary plans increase your options and your confidence and are clear, inspiring stories for employees to rally around. Evolutionary plans leverage organizational interdependence and cross-departmental synergy by ensuring that strategic objectives are always organizational in nature – not departmental. *(Jan's mentor communicated to her that not only do they need to be organizational, but that they need to be directly connected to a compelling customer-focused value proposition.)* Finally, Evolutionary plans identify measurable areas of improvement that are directly related to problem solving and the real world tactical challenges faced day-to-day within the organization. So, Jan sees an end-to-end connection (ideally) between the guiding value proposition – organizational focus and priorities – and the net results that make a difference for the bottom line.

It's moving beyond organizational strategy to a strong value-driven relationship to the customer moves a good organization to a truly Evolutionary organization. Two great examples of this are Travel Oregon and Bluetooth SIG and their masterful work in building partnerships for better customer relationships.

Travel Oregon

Todd Davidson and Scott West of Travel Oregon know a thing or two about the relationship between good planning and great partnerships. Travel Oregon was one of the first organizations to pioneer the Meta-Planning concept.

TODD DAVIDSON: *You need to have a great strategic plan and clear mission so that you can go out and give partners a reason to come together with you. There has to be a common vision. We knew that in order to reach our goals there was an interdependency that was needed and it had to be nurtured, so we worked really, really hard to do that. We held public forums, conducted surveys, asked a lot of questions. And then we went out to two thousand of our industry partners and asked them questions about how they are working, what they were doing and how we could give them skin in the* *game. Then we rolled our plan out at a state-wide conference to share the details and give people a lot of time to respond before we implemented the plan officially. Then we did follow-up calls, posted the plan on our website in a way that was simple and easy to digest, and allowed the public to comment real time. That is one common mistake – to make your communication too long – to give people a plan that is like the Encyclopedia Britannica.*

SCOTT WEST: *We treat partnerships as a long-term investment. You may be before a legislative committee one day and things don't go your way and folks you are representing want to storm the castle and burn the thing down, but you know that you may be right back in front of that committee again tomorrow on a different issue, so you have to be measured. From a leadership perspective you truly understand that you cannot do anything except through your partners. Travel Oregon has done that really well.*

The Power of Partnerships for Evolutionary Planning

Evolutionary Planning that places partnerships at the center often involves inviting potential partners (and even industry competitors) to the table to participate in the planning process. We call this kind of planning Meta-Planning. Meta-Planning is a methodology for creating shared, developmental priorities among individuals, boards, agencies, and businesses who recognize the inexorable interdependence of their futures – looking out to a 10- or even 20-year horizon. The resulting plan will describe a preferred end state or goal along with three distinct shared progress milestones to encourage adjustment and adaptation along the way. While a meta-planning process can be initiated by anyone, it is owned by no one except the actual participants in the process. Key outcomes of a meta-planning process include:

- Agreement on general term definitions, variables, and constraints shared by the larger group;
- Development of an "aspire to" vision that would not be possible without the ongoing cooperation of the larger group; and
- Development and use of shared communication and influence collateral that will be used by individual stakeholders to guide their own planning, outreach, and lobbying efforts.

A big theme with Travel Oregon is the ability to create interdependent relationships with people and partners that in any other situation would either not be paying any attention to one another or would have an adversarial relationship with one another. As a part of their planning, Travel Oregon was able to bring together trade groups, state and federal government representatives, the Bureau of Land Management and other various entities and bring them to the table as if that's all just supposed to happen. When you go to a Travel Oregon Trade Conference or something like that you are struck by the fact that there are all the people there who in another situation could easily see themselves across the table from one another in a very contentious and adversarial way and here you have them all holding the chorus book, dressed real nicely and singing in three-part harmony.

Bluetooth SIG

Bluetooth SIG's business is defined by the strength of its partner relationships. It's how the business was built, how it will grow, and how it will continue to change the world. Meta-Planning was not just some new fad in strategic planning to try – for Bluetooth SIG, there was never any other option.

MIKE FOLEY: *It is something that always amazes me when I go to a meeting and there is Nokia, Motorola, Samsung, Sony Ericsson – all the big mobile phone manufacturers talking and openly communicating and working together to get a specification out the door and then they know that that they are going to be fierce competitors within the market. But they do that because they know that they need some base level functionality for the consumer that works with their competitors, so that the competitor's headset you already own will still work with their phone they want you to buy. I think, that's the biggest thing that people underestimate is how hard it is to create the eco-system so that the technology can add value to all the participants in it and not just the one that created the phone. That is what Bluetooth is about.*

Mike Foley is heart and mind a "tech" guy. He may have his PhD in Engineering, but he is operating in a leadership environment that is highly political, competitive and sophisticated. And there are a lot of soft skills he has had to apply to be successful in building key partnerships every day. Mike talks to everyone in the industry and makes sure to understand each perspective. He is systematic in getting feedback from each partner. That's how he is able to make inferences about what people are saying and what they aren't saying to put together a picture and a process for moving ahead.

Meta-Planning

In both the Bluetooth SIG and Travel Oregon examples above, we see the role of the Evolutionary plan as the spark plug for the internal organizational engine as well as the ever-important external partner and customer relationships that drive success and loyalty. Their plans are shaping not just their own companies, but an entire ecosystem of business over decades for the mutual benefit of all. That's the real power behind great Meta-Planning – Evolutionary Plans that have the potential to change not only companies and industries, but the world.

Some other great examples of Meta-Planning that results in Evolutionary Plans:

- A plan that invites public agencies, prevention care providers, educators and citizen groups to significantly reduce the pervasiveness and cost of chronic, preventable disease in an area.
- A plan that invites credit unions and bankers, operational enemies – to sit down and develop a shared set of legislative priorities for the upcoming decade and to find a way to approach state and national lobbying efforts with an actionable vision.
- A plan that allows manufacturers, marketers, consumer groups and retailers to establish an entirely new market segment, quality agenda or customer satisfaction system.

The essential characteristic that distinguishes the Meta-Planning process from other types of strategic planning is the explicit recognition that, no matter what, we are – at some level – in this together. And to that extent, at the very least, our plans should be public.

Truly, Evolutionary plans are magic beans that most organizations throw away or de-value. The organizations that will win in the future are those that realize the huge potential of these short, compelling, public-facing "invitations" to a new way to think and work in the global economy.

CHAPTER 3
Evolutionary Leadership

Evolutionary Wisdom

Mountains could be made from books that have been written on the topic of leadership. Some are great, some are terrible, some are based in theory and some focus on more practical experience and application. We have read many of them and believe that you should too. This chapter is not about defining all that is good or necessary when it comes to leading organizations. Instead, we focus on the specific characteristics that distinguish those leaders who consistently and effectively lead transformational change in their organizations from all the other excellent leaders that also exist in business today.

Again, we stress that Evolutionary Leaders are not necessarily the best leaders. Some organizations need to remain stable, weather a storm, or even phase out specific lines of business. New ideas, innovation and transformative change would be foolhardy endeavors. In these cases, the last thing you need is an Evolutionary Leader. But, for those organizations that need to transform, implement big changes, innovate or find new ways to survive and thrive, read on for more wisdom from our Evolutionary Leaders.

Scott West starts by explaining that Evolutionary Leaders are driven by a passion for what they do. This passion is authentic. There is no "CEO talent search" strategy that will work to find the latest *Forbes* cover executive and offer him or her millions to be your Evolutionary. Evolutionary Leaders are, by definition, emotionally committed to the cause they pursue.

SCOTT WEST: *Todd Davidson makes what he does at Travel Oregon look really easy and I think it is because of the preparation and the hard work that he puts in behind the scenes. He really has passion for the State and his keen insight on the heart of the State and what really beats here makes it easy for him to convey that to people who want to work here. Todd could choose to do anything he wants but he chooses this because he loves this State and I think he loves the people he gets to do this with.*

Todd Davidson has committed his career to leading Travel Oregon through transformational change because he is personally invested in the travel industry's success in Oregon. He believes in the work, the mission, and the potential. Cindy Tortorici would say that he knows his "Why"…

CINDY TORTORICI: *Just as your organizational strategy depends on Why, How and What, so does your personal leadership strategy. The best leaders need to be self-aware and know the Why behind their leadership. Think about your Why as being your motivator for doing the work that you choose to do. It takes time to work on ourselves and it can be a daunting task, but if we don't have our own house in order we cannot lead others effectively. When we know ourselves we stand a little taller; we become more confident. We are better able to collaborate, participate, step up and volunteer our strengths, and admit when we don't know something. We are more authentic, and more comfortable with who we are. People are drawn to and will follow that kind of leader.*

Evolutionary Leaders are definitely authentic. They are comfortable with who they are, and they know why they do what they do. They have committed a piece of themselves to their work – are willing to tie their hearts as well as their minds to the outcomes of their teams and organizations. Cindy goes on to explain how knowing our Why makes us more courageous – a key component of Evolutionary Leadership, as these leaders constantly pioneer new territory and take chances on the unknown.

CINDY TORTORICI: *Your Why represents your values. I gave a presentation on this topic a few years ago and a man came up to me afterward and said, "Cindy, I'm worried about my Why… I think I just love money." I said to him, "Hey, there's nothing wrong with money. But I can tell you right now that money is not your Why. If it were just about money, then you could go sell drugs. Why don't you do that? The reason you don't is because of your values. So, there is more to your Why than just money. Think about your values and what brings you joy in this job and throughout your life, and you will get to your Why."*

Once Evolutionary Leaders are liberated by knowing their Why, they can accomplish truly extraordinary things. Part of the secret to accomplishing great things is to proudly exclaim to the public what you are attempting to achieve. Most leaders, even very good leaders, are not comfortable sharing their dreams with the world. But Geoff Gilmore has no hesitation when it comes to sharing his values as an Evolutionary Leader.

GEOFF GILMORE: *My mission as CEO is to provide an extraordinary life for the people who work at Climax Portable Machine Tools. This means an extraordinary work life and an extraordinary personal life. There is a pervasive line of thought in management that people are supposed to leave their home life at home and their work life at work. No personal calls at work, and no work calls or talking about work at home. But this is not how we really work as human beings. We don't just shut off our families, our children and loved ones when we go to work, and we don't stop thinking about work when we are at home – especially when we love what we do. How many times have you solved a work problem while doing something creative or fun at home with your family? We _want_ people to think about work when they are at home – that is often the time when they are the most rested, the most relaxed, and able to think of the most innovative solutions.*

Not only is Geoff enthusiastic when he talks about the power of investing in the happiness of his people, he understands that is it just this kind of risk that reaps high business returns. Geoff is a master of systems thinking and he utilizes his knowledge extensively in the workflows and processes at Climax. In other words, he doesn't just get people – he gets how to create the kind of environment that encourages the best from those people every day. At Climax, engineers are asked to solve problems like fixing the Hoover Dam or building new underwater methods for repairing Navy SEAL submarines. The stakes are high, and failure is costly in more devastating ways than the loss of profits. Geoff makes big bets on his people. And they make big miracles happen every day.

At Travel Oregon, Evolutionary Leaders Todd Davidson and Scott West have a similar philosophy.

SCOTT WEST: *Jobs in our organization are cherished because we work to create a place where people can thrive. People really want to be here because Todd has helped define a mission that they see as important, and he allows them to bloom. He encourages us to accept the responsibility of this work and accept the personal and professional growth that comes from doing that and having success with that. It is easy to reach over the top of somebody if you know better and say "no you need to do it this way," but it is much more effective if folks come to that on their own. That is a skill set that is rare and the ability to be comfortable with the organization's future and essentially trusting his own future in the hands of the rest of us is an important thing. I think that is a rare gift and to me it all boils down to people.*

The bet Todd Davidson is taking is that through the shared values of a commitment to travel and tourism in the state of Oregon, his team will do it right. He takes the risk of leaving his own reputation in the hands of his team not just because he believes in them, but because he knows that this "pledge" of good faith on his part is a strong motivator for his team to commit to his leadership and the mission. Could he get burned? Absolutely. But it is precisely this sort of risk on people and passion that sets

Evolutionary Leaders apart. To them such leaps of faith constitute "just another day at the office."

Chandra Brown clarifies that while Evolutionary Leaders are experts at giving their power away in the form of trusting and empowering teams, they are also unwavering in their commitment to step up and take the lead when tough decisions need to be made.

CHANDRA BROWN: *One of the worst things leaders can do is shirk their role to make decisions for the team – especially in times of uncertainty and disruption. If a leader shirks his or her decision-making it slows momentum, and delays outcomes if not prohibits them. When leaders don't step up and make the tough decisions in a timely way it causes a great deal more chaos for the team. In fact, it is more dangerous to have a leader that won't make those calls than for the team to have no leader at all. In the ideal world the team moves forward and life is great and the leader really doesn't have to do much. But there will always be times when a leader needs to come in and make the hard decision. Everyone is waiting for direction. Leaders don't know everything, and often you need to make the decision without having the "perfect" answer. So you have to do what you believe is right. If a leader does not step in and do something then you just have this swirling mass of a "team" expending energy uselessly because they are no longer moving for-ward, growing more frustrated and dissatisfied with their work, less willing to cooperate and more likely to move toward solutions that are less ideal. That's why it is so critical that leaders actually* <u>*lead*</u>*.*

Evolutionary Leaders are not afraid to make these "final" deci-sions – the calls that no one else is willing to make. But they will often put the decision off until the last possible moment in the hope that the team will emerge with an answer first. Evolutionary Leaders are committed to team engagement and grassroots ideation to a fault – they know that this is what drives the best innovation. But Evolutionary Leaders also know that teams need a leader – and the only real reason that is true is to forward actions through one source for critical decisions. Cindy Tortorici expands on this notion of the Evolutionary Leader as a decision-maker and what can happen to teams where decisions are delayed for too long.

CINDY TORTORICI: *When leaders don't make final decisions it creates a team environment that is plagued by conflict. Some leaders think this is a good thing – that it makes for stronger teams. But in my experience this theory rarely works in practice. Conflict in the workplace or between managers of a company should not be thought of as a "culture" that is sustainable. Unending conflict, constant clash, doesn't make people stronger, it wears them out. Placing your best people in situations of constant conflict will only serve to burn out your best people. The strongest leaders are those who are willing to shut conflict down when necessary. Put an end to it. Leaders make final decisions. That's part of the job. So, ask for advice, ask lots of questions, gather lots of data, and debate and seek out conflicting advice, but in the end, you have to be willing to make a final decision. Someone has to lead, point out the non-negotiable direction and allow people to move forward because never-ending conflict makes for bad business strategy.*

It is likely that in times of significant organizational transformation that your people will have to operate in an environment that is unstable, unpredictable, and in flux. Demands will be placed on them for increased flexibility, responsiveness, and adaptability. In short, they will be under stress. In this phase of "controlled chaos" Evolutionary Leaders know that conflict can easily move from positive clash to unhealthy exercises in politicking, back-stabbing and gossip. These leaders also know that to keep the clash positive they need to continuously elevate the challenge (raise the bar for excellence) and make the timely decisions necessary to speed progress along at a strong clip.

Why You Need Evolutionary Leaders

The grand potential of strategy is the ability to be intentional and opportunistic about your organization's future. It is about thinking about your company in one year, five years, 10 years, 30 years. An

Evolutionary Leader is necessary if change is a vital component of your future strategic success. The more change you see in your organization's future, the more Evolutionary Leaders you need. For example, we believe that health care will dramatically grow in its demand for Evolutionary Leadership in the next decade as the industry transforms the way it serves patients and achieves fiscal soundness. And, as we said before, there are also companies that do not need Evolutionary Leaders. If your organization has been making the same widget for 50 years and will continue to do so for 50 more in basically the same way – you may not need an Evolutionary leader. In fact, in organizations that are trying not to change Evolutionary Leaders can be detrimental.

Perhaps the biggest reason to have an Evolutionary Leader in your organization is because strategic challenges demand strategic solutions. By definition that means that traditional siloed leadership is dysfunctional. An Evolutionary Leader is able to create mission clarity and urgency between and among disparate organizational resources and partners.

How Evolutionaries Lead

In his last years, C.K. Prahalad, Professor of Strategy at the University of Michigan Ross School of Business, taught his students that the best leaders "...understand the importance of nonconformity. Leadership is about change, hope, and the future. Leaders have to venture into uncharted territory, so they must be able to handle intellectual solitude and ambiguity." In other words, leaders often feel lonely. Evolutionary Leaders cope well with such loneliness because they know who they are and believe deeply in what they are trying to accomplish. It is such a sense of conviction that allows Evolutionary Leaders to persevere in the face of countless failed ideas, strategies, projects, and prototypes. It's this unique combination of confidence, drive and compassion that enables Evolutionary Leaders to gather followers and get things done.

Evolutionary Leaders:
- *Possess "Street Credibility"*
- *Know who they are*
- *Garner trust, respect and followers*
- *Will make final decisions*

There is no doubt that Evolutionary leaders know their business. Whether they possess a great deal of formal education, lots of on-the-job experience, or a heaping helping of both – one thing is certain, inside of their organizations, Evolutionary leaders **possess "street credibility."** We recognize that the elements that make one credible differ depending on the type of business. For example, in a science lab, having a PhD in Neuroscience might be your calling card for gaining respect. But it would mean very little in a mechanic's shop where they repair cars for a living. So, when we talk about *street credibility* in your business, we simply mean that the people in your organization firmly believe that you know what you are talking about. Are you qualified to lead in your company? Are you able to judge the quality of other kinds of information and communications? We are talking about the premise that your ability to lead people through transformational change is a function of the perceived credibility of your position, your strategies, your presentations, your emails… you get the idea. This may sound like common sense, and it is, but you might be surprised how many leaders we see that are missing this critical component of Evolutionary leadership. We learn from Scott West that at Travel Oregon, Todd Davidson has gained credibility through his field experience, knowledge about the travel industry, and perhaps most important, his ability and willingness to share this knowledge with others.

Evolutionary leaders know who they are – as Cindy Tortorici tells us, they know their "Why." Sure, you could easily argue that this kind of self-awareness is the subject of a whole other book – or even a religion, maybe! But that is the power of reflected appraisal. Reflected appraisal is the phenomenon of mirroring the judgments of the people around you. And the judgments of the significant others around you have more weight. It is not that your identity is a function of the people around you, it is that your identity is a function of the *significance that you give* to what the people around you say. As you develop your Evolutionary competencies, you are less and less reliant on the opinions of others to compose your own identity and sense of right or wrong, good work or bad work, correct behavior or incorrect behavior. For more in-depth study of this evolutionary development we recommend reading the works of Robert Kegan, PhD, a professor of Psychology at Harvard University. Dr. Kegan describes this progressive growth as moving through "orders of mind." The point is that we are always comparing ourselves to those around us, but each of us is influenced in different ways and to differing degrees by these observations. This is one of those areas where Evolutionary Leaders stand out from other leaders because they are able to act without requiring as much validation from the society around them. In fact they may see too much validation as a sign that they are not "doing their job" as well as they should be. The key thing to remember is that you are in control of with whom you are comparing yourself. How high do you look? Where do you identify your "peers" in leadership? Evolutionary leaders may not find appropriate comparisons in those nearest to them – sometimes you have to look beyond your social sphere to find leaders that make good comparisons.

Evolutionary leaders are also comfortable with the notion of having more than one leadership "identity" – that there are times when they will step back and hand over authority to someone else on the team. The Evolutionary leader is able to adapt and create a collaborative leadership identity so that everyone in the organization is legitimately participating in the *construction* of the leadership identity, and that is not seen as a threat to the Evolutionary leader. Because at the end of the day, the Evolutionary leader is a construct in much the same way that Generals, with all the badges and insignias of rank, are self-delusional when they think they are fundamentally different than anyone else. They play a role. Sure, not everyone can play that role well, but it is the role that is a function of a social construction that depends on everyone around them to uphold that construction. The day people don't buy-in anymore is the day the illusion is dispelled. And that leads to our next point.

Evolutionary Leaders have mastered the ability to *garner trust, respect and followers.* Any good strategy will have a reliable road map. Taking people off the beaten path to achieve change or innovation is all well and good, but there must still be a path. People follow leaders who know where they are going and are unwavering in their commitment to reach the end state. Evolutionary leaders foster confidence because they know who they are and they have a strong emotional commitment to the vision – this stability in the wake of change and innovation (fundamentally instable forces) is the key to building trust, respect and followers. At the end of the day what people want from a leader is to know two things: do you have a plan and are you going to take me with you?

Chandra Brown's story teaches us that momentum is an essential part of the evolutionary experience and that means Evolutionary leaders *will make final decisions* to keep the team moving ahead at all times. Evolutionary leaders make judgment calls and people rely on them to be experienced and intelligent in making tough decisions. Chandra touches on a key point of leadership: decision-making. Teams are really looking for action, teams are really looking for something to do, so at some point, every good leader has to be comfortable with stopping a conversation and saying "Okay, I have heard what all of you have to say, now here is what we are going to do. This is the next step, and this is the step after that." Chandra teaches us that Evolutionary leaders "constantly deliver." Evolutionary leaders understand that successful leadership depends on reliability, and that sort of credibility, once earned, is not guaranteed forever. You have to constantly replenish the account.

C H A P T E R 4

Evolutionary Communication

Evolutionary Wisdom

Communication is the key to establishing our competencies and talents and to demonstrating our sincerity. Evolutionary Communicators know the value of authentic communication when it comes to driving transformational change. Authenticity is a term that has been overused in the past few years when talking about everything from leadership to branding to sales. What we mean by authenticity is that Evolutionary Communicators place their *motive* at the center of their communication efforts. The presence of human motive is the root of action – it's what motivates ourselves and those around us to commit to a course and achieve results. When Evolutionary Communicators place motive at the center of their communication efforts, they achieve clarity. Others are better able to understand the Evolutionary Communicator's driving values and purpose for acting. This communication behavior is exactly what people are referring to when they talk about someone's "integrity."

Whether you call it authenticity, honesty, being straight-forward, or just a "straight-shooter" – motive-led communication is at the heart of transformative change. Scott West shares an example of how this sort of honest communication changed the game for Travel Oregon.

SCOTT WEST: When I look back at the planning, the process, the research, the policy work, and the strong partnerships, such an incredible amount of trust was needed. The honest conversations across the table about how to impact the future and how to not waste the opportunity in a recession took a huge effort. We found a way to drive the economic opportunity but we still had to bring all the people to the table to have these important conversations across the whole industry. We knew that we would have to start those conversations – put our neck out there first and say what needed to be said. I think the key is to be proactive – to share what you know, what you believe, and to have courage enough to say, "We think the future is going to look like this so we are going to plant our flag out in front of that."

Through a series of tough, "get real" conversations Travel Oregon was able to bring together businesses, agencies and non-profits across the state to align around a shared vision for travel and tourism in the next several decades. The trick was to keep their motive for introducing change clear and compelling throughout the process.

Evolutionary Communicators are not only masters of authentic dialogue, they know they are willing to error on the side of "over" communicating when it comes to sharing information and soliciting feedback from employees, teams, stakeholders and partners – as Mike Foley demonstrates in his approach to communication.

*MIKE FOLEY: A good leader in this industry is going to make sure to talk with **everyone**. You can't just go out and plan based on what the mobile phone industry needs. You need to also understand what the headphone manufacturers need, what the auto designers need, and what the PC folks need, and you can't get the whole picture from any one of them. You have to talk to all of them and pull it all together. The story you get may not always be as well defined as it should be, but you have to be willing to get out there and meet with people, because they aren't always going to be beating down your door to come and talk with you. And once you have that picture, you have to bounce it off your team, your employees and bring them into the dialogue. It can be exhausting – but I know of no better way to succeed in this marketplace.*

If inclusive communication is critical on the front end of planning and design, it is just as important to debrief. Evolutionary Communicators are quick to check in with teams after projects and milestones to find out what went well and what needs to be better. They know that in fast-paced change, high performance teams can't afford to repeat mistakes. The Navy SEALs offer one of the best approaches to soliciting rapid post-project feedback.

CAPTAIN STEVE AHLBERG: *It is critical to debrief after each mission. I believe debriefing has to be done immediately after whatever the mission is so lessons are not lost. The SEAL Teams routinely debrief immediately after an operation before cleaning up or anything else. Debriefing captures the lessons learned, the things we could do better, the things we did well. We record all lessons learned immediately, while it is fresh. If you wait then you tend to forget or minimize those things that could be most critical. Thorough debriefing is the last thing most people want to do upon completion of an operation, but you have to do it. Sometimes we would come back to a submarine and share containers of ice cream, some hamburgers, etc., so we could eat and relax while we did the debrief. The point is you need to do it immediately because that is where you will capture the most important lessons.*

Evolutionary Communicators realize that the more significant the change, the faster things are moving, the more important communication becomes. But how many organizations have the discipline to debrief project teams within 24 hours of the project conclusion? It is exactly this sort of commitment that keeps organizations on track for positive transformation to occur. And when you create an environment where good communication is the norm, where people can speak with authenticity, and share their motives openly – you create a culture that people are willing to invest in. Geoff Gilmore explains how that investment works to create an organizational reputation that most organizations don't achieve.

GEOFF GILMORE: *Knowing our values as a company and communicating those values consistently in the stories we tell, the actions we take, and the* *messaging we design has worked over time to create a "word on the street" about what it's like to work at Climax that has extended into the community. And it is remarkable. I remember we had a guy who was driving into town for an interview with us and he had trouble finding the location. So he stopped at a local gas station and asked the attendant if he knew the address. The attendant said he had no idea where that address was. The man replied that he was going to an interview at Climax and hoped not to be late. The attendant remarked, "Oh, Climax? I know where that is – I just didn't know the address! That place is supposed to be a great company to work for, if they offer you a job you should really think about taking it!" We love that people we have never met are ambassadors for our company. You cannot buy that kind of reputation.*

Evolutionary Communicators like Geoff understand that their employees are "whole people" – that they tell the stories from their work at home, to relatives and friends, out at bars and in coffee shops, and those stories are powerful. And Evolutionary Communicators are intentional about constructing the kind of stories that "ring true" for people – that inspire, motivate, and compel.

Finally Chandra Brown reminds us that Evolutionary Communication is often different for women executives. But regardless of the style, the purpose remains the same – to be authentic, clear, and inspire action.

CHANDRA BROWN: *Some of the most valuable lessons I have learned during my career at Oregon Iron Works center around communication. I have found that women, in general, communicate in different ways from men. And since I work mainly with men, that could have been a barrier for me. So I had to learn how to communicate in the way that could lead people forward and inspire them. Obviously, if I could not articulate a viable message, I would never be able to implement my ideas. But successful leadership is also about action. What you are going to be judged on is how well what you said is going to be translated into what you do. It's great to communicate the idea of building a streetcar but it is not until the streetcar is built and people are riding on it, and it's safe and it's effective, that you really* *have credibility with your teams and your community. Credibility is about constantly delivering on what you say you will deliver. But credibility has to be continually refreshed. You are always continually working and as soon as we stop then I think credibility begins to fade. I have found that direct and clear communication is incredibly helpful because it gets to the heart of the matter – it cuts through the concepts and ideas to the part where people are actually going to do something. You have to make it simple and communicate an action plan because people want to be doing things – they want to be pointed in a direction of action. They feel more vested than if they are just talking about something.*

Chandra gives us two important lessons here: 1) Communication is about spurring people to *action* – transformative change requires that people translate ideas into reality, and 2) Evolutionary Communicators know how to adapt their message and style to their audience to make an impact.

Why You Need Evolutionary Communicators

An Evolutionary Communicator is like a master of communication aikido. Aikido is a martial art form based in the belief that you can defend yourself by effectively using the energy and momentum of your opponent rather than generating new energy. Most leaders we meet tell us that communication in their organizations is really tough – that it takes a ton of energy and time. So, inevitably people slack off on good communication practices because they feel that doing it well is just too hard. It's like constantly swimming upstream. But we believe that even when you *stop* communicating, you are saying something. If you buy the premise that you cannot opt out of communicating (even not communicating will be interpreted by others as having some sort of meaning), then it is actually impossible to not communicate. So if you can't not communicate, then the question is: what are you communicating? Where Evolutionary Communicators stand out is that they can use the current mechanisms and traditions of the organization's communication culture to introduce or reinforce key strategic messages – especially messages around change and transformation. This is what we see Chandra Brown doing when she adapts her messaging style to a bunch of male engineers who need to build world-class streetcars.

It is essential in any organization that negative feedback flow easily so that problems and choke points in a plan can be addressed quickly. The Evolutionary Communicator is the organic, informal message sender that can name and recognize the reality of what is happening in the field and generate an effective feedback loop to top leadership that is mission-critical for any strategy's success. This is just what the Navy SEALs are doing when they conduct rapid debriefing after a mission. The practice has been established, and it has become part of the culture itself. It would be hard *not* to do it.

When you have Evolutionary Communicators monitoring and driving your strategic messaging, your organization can achieve transformative change faster and with more lasting success as new ways of exchanging, sharing and funneling information become ingrained in the very nature of how work gets done.

How Evolutionaries Communicate

Research conducted by Sandy Pentland of MIT's Human Dynamics Lab, published in the *Harvard Business Review* in January 2010, shows that the more successful people are more energetic communicators – that "It's not what you say, it's how you say it." The study used established science to predict with an 87% degree of accuracy which executives would win a business competition or sales pitch solely on the basis of the social signals they send. Devices that recorded data on their social signals – tone of voice, gesticulation, proximity to others and more – predicted each winner without reading or hearing the actual pitches." (Note: judges that only read the pitches chose different winners.)

The winning executives talked more than those that were not

so successful. But the study showed the key difference between the winners and the losers was that the winning executives also *listened* more. By talking more – sharing their stories and asking lots of questions – they were better able to elicit responses from others. And when people responded, they listened closely. From these conversations they gathered feedback, learned preferences, and spent time really getting to know people. They put a lot of themselves out there, and they got a lot in return. Perhaps the most interesting outcome of the study was the discovery that the more of these sorts of people that were placed together on a team the better that team performed.

Evolutionary Communicators are a lot like the executives in the study described above. They understand that communication is not just about transferring information – but about building relationships and garnering support to achieve positive outcomes. We see Evolutionary communication as the need to express influence, and to be an agent of leadership and change in the organization. It is about making great presentations, managing meetings effectively, writing great e-mails and positively participating in the hundreds of informal conversations that take place each week. It is an expression of action and deliberation. Philosopher Kenneth Burke would call this an "impulse to action."

Evolutionary Communicators:
- *Are inclusive*
- *Constantly refine*
- *Are effective*
- *Use media-centered strategies*

The Evolutionary Communicator is ***inclusive,*** using a broad palate of resources and voices, a wide array of research and data, and a lot of people. Evolutionary Communicators are comfortable getting a lot of "fingerprints" on a process and broadening the dialogue early in the process. Yes, that does mean projects can take longer. But the results will become a more lasting and effective component of the organization's culture. Evolutionaries know that when you build people into the processes and the strategy, you have a stronger foundation from which you can grow, innovate and lead as an organization.

Evolutionary Communicators take responsibility for "netting" out major points and *refining* themes from the conversations they are in. They see it as their job. They can quickly and easily take the 20 pages of dialogue and create one slide that synthesizes and refines the salient issues. And they know how to use this talent to gather buy-in, rally the troops and get things done. They become the "go to" leaders in their organizations because they have the valuable information people need and are willing to share what they know in ways that teach others and build community. Refining, at its core, is about creating clarity. And Evolutionary Communicators know that clarity is what teams need to stay motivated, keep momentum, and reach a desirable end state. One of the most effective ways to achieve clarity and gain influence with others is to use the power of narrative – to tell a good story. In his book, *Simplicity*, Bill Jensen explains that if you want to create clarity you have to look for something that defines a common meaning for everyone. Evolutionary Communicators know that "something" is storytelling. They are masters at

- Moving beyond the data to tell the larger, value-based story
- Connecting that goal at hand to the larger strategic vision
- Using great metaphors or every-day comparisons to explain the "heart" of an idea
- Using the story to cut through the noise of everyday business to quickly make the complex clear

And perhaps most importantly, the Evolutionary Communicator knows how to give that message back to the ecosystem from which it came. They don't claim ownership of the dialogue or its outcomes, but see themselves as a facilitator and refiner of the conversation that already belongs to the community of stakeholders involved. Easily communicating without needing to have the power or control over the communication is what makes Evolutionaries so *effective*. A key lesson in Chandra Brown's story is how she excelled in leadership by learning the language of the culture she was working in. Her ability to become fluent in the language of the engineers at Oregon Iron Works allowed her to quickly build her credibility, demonstrate her understanding of the company's challenges and opportunities and sell her ideas. Clear and refined communication worked to keep momentum going and to ensure that goals were achieved, which was essential for building credibility.

Media-Centered

The Evolutionary Communicator is completely aware that in the best case scenario the message is going out as widely as possible. They create buy-in, they spread messages. They always err on the side of more transparency. They are not afraid of sharing and over-sharing. They are not good corporate secret-keepers. They are going to be thinking of building walking decks and short videos and interview pieces to share the vision, educate people and garner followers through a narrative that people can rally around. They use messages to create alignment. They use media to be even more inclusive, to actively empower more people to join the conversation – thus the media acts as an invitation to the conversation. But the media is also critical because it helps to ensure the consistency of the conversation; it controls the message so that everyone in the conversation is using the same language to engage in the dialogue.

- *Note: it is a given assumption that the media has a short shelf-life. This is not about high-end marketing pieces, but the day-to-day methods of utilizing in-house resources to create media "on the go" that can be used in real time.*

You will recall that one of the lessons we take from Chandra

Brown's experience is that Evolutionary Communicators know how to adapt their message and style to their audience to make an impact. The best way to adapt to your audience is to have a solid understanding of how you communicate naturally, and how your audience prefers to communicate. In other words, you need to know about Communication Orientations.

Communication Orientation

A significant amount of research in the area of Social Cognition confirms the idea that people see the characteristics of "successful" communication very differently. For example, some people see conflict as a sign of trouble. Others see conflict as a natural and expected part of social interaction – it is normal, even healthy. If you learn about these characteristics, you will understand yourself better and you will be able to better understand the point of view (or "orientation") that others bring to their communications. Researchers use three different categories to describe our basic communication orientation:

Direct

- Direct communicators **say what they think** – and they don't necessarily think about how others will receive the message. They don't mind conflict and see conflict as a natural part of communicating.
- Direct communicators don't view communication as being all that complicated. They believe that they have communicated effectively when they have a thought, and they say it.
- Direct communicators are consistent in their approach. They don't change their behaviors much from one situation to the next.
- Direct communicators may not attend to all the rules of polite conversation. And they do not necessarily value all of those rules when others speak to them.

Situational

- Situational communicators believe that we will all get along a lot better if we all **know our roles**, and **follow the rules**.
- Situational communicators believe that they have communicated effectively when they say or do the right thing for the specific situation. These people align their communication with conventional roles and strive to say what is "appropriate" in a given situation.
- Situational communicators tend to be very concerned about how other people feel, and they see conflict as a problem.
- Situational communicators like to know all of the expectations that are present in a given situation so that they can be prepared and appropriate.

Bonding

- Bonding communicators are interested in whatever the **other person** is interested in. This is not an insincere interest. They will talk about mountain climbing for an hour with someone who is interested in mountain climbing – even though they have shown no interest in it themselves in the past.
- Bonding communicators believe they have communicated successfully when they have created a bond with the person with whom they are speaking.
- Bonding communicators tend to downplay formal rules and roles if it will help build a better bond. They might say, for example, "Don't think of me as your manager…" in order to elevate the person-to-person relationship.
- Bonding communicators adapt to every person they speak with, so their communication style will change a lot – even in a single situation.

Know Your Communication Orientation

Self-awareness with regard to how we craft our messages is an essential step in enhancing our communication so that others can actually hear us more clearly. What's more, when we know our own tendencies we can better comprehend and contend with the tendencies of those around us so that we, in turn, can hear them without our own defensive reactions getting in the way.

So get out your Number Two pencils and prepare to take a quick quiz. Answer honestly – reflecting not the way you'd *like* to be, or the way you're trying to be, but the way you are. Remember, there is no "best" way to be and no organization could survive without people who fall into all three categories: Bonding, Situational and Direct.

Quiz

Please circle the number (5–1) that best corresponds to your thinking about each of the fifteen statements listed below:

5 – strongly agree   4 – agree   3 – neutral   2 – disagree   1 – strongly disagree

1.	I am a "get to the point" kind of person.	5	4	3	2	1
2.	I like to know the details about what is expected in work situations.	5	4	3	2	1
3.	If I am in a good conversation, I can stay focused even in a noisy or busy atmosphere.	5	4	3	2	1
4.	People describe me as being very consistent.	5	4	3	2	1
5.	I work best when I know what role I am supposed to play and the roles that others are supposed to play.	5	4	3	2	1
6.	I don't have to actually be personally involved in something to be interested in it; I like to hear about mountain climbing – even though I am not a climber myself.	5	4	3	2	1

7.	It is best to be direct when you are offering criticism or bad news.	5	4	3	2	1
8.	I try to respect other people's points of view when I am in conversation with them even if I don't agree.	5	4	3	2	1
9.	It is very satisfying to meet people and develop a genuine connection with them.	5	4	3	2	1
10.	Conflict is a natural part of communication; you just have to deal with it as best you can.	5	4	3	2	1
11.	Communication is based on reciprocity, give and take, working together.	5	4	3	2	1
12.	People describe me as being very adaptive; I make friends quickly.	5	4	3	2	1
13.	In general there is too much chitchat and pointless conversation in the workplace.	5	4	3	2	1
14.	The best managers set out very clear expectations and organizational rules.	5	4	3	2	1
15.	The key to communication is personal empathy and being able to connect with the other person's point of view.	5	4	3	2	1

Scoring the Quiz

The statements on this quiz speak to a series of different approaches to business communication. The key statements focus on a series of communication styles defined as:

- *Direct*
- *Situational*
- *Bonding*

To score your quiz:

- Calculate your total for items 1, 4, 7, 10, and 13. This is your Direct Score.
- Calculate your total for items 2, 5, 8, 11, and 15. This is your Situational Score.
- Calculate your total for items 3, 6, 9, 12, and 14. This is your Bonding Score.

Interpreting Your Results

These communication orientations are based in part on a significant body of research in communication theory begun by Dr. Jesse Delia at the University of Illinois. The nice thing about this work is that it does not seem to be dependent on gender, socioeconomic status, or education; the theory gets at the "basic" assumptions that shape our approach to communication.

If you have a high Direct score, then you are most likely very comfortable with your approach to communication and you are probably wondering what all of the fuss is about.

If you have a high Situational score, then you are probably attuned to situational cues. You are probably very perceptive and sensitive to the dynamics from one situation to the next. You appreciate clarity in communication and roles. You work hard to make sure that feelings are not hurt.

If you have a high Bonding score, you are probably what others would call a "people person." You value making connection with others. You have a wide range of interests and you see great conversation as an end in and of itself.

If you have several high scores, you are probably Bonding with a "preferred" approach that is Situational or Direct. The theory suggests that Bonding speakers have the capacity to access any of the styles, and that Situational speakers can access the Direct style – though they probably feel uncomfortable if they are forced to be Direct. Direct speakers are happy being just the way they are. Use these scores as general indicators of your stylistic preferences.

Please read on to learn more about your communication

orientation in terms of its strong points and potential pitfalls. But – and this is crucial – be sure to read about the other two categories as well if you are interested in being able to communicate clearly to everyone in every situation.

Direct Speakers

What's So Great About Direct Speakers?

There are many advantages to being a Direct speaker. Everyone knows where they stand with you, and even if they don't like where they stand, this is actually a quite valuable thing to know. Unlike those bonding chameleons, you are also extremely consistent in what you say and how you say it. Everyone is well aware of who will show up and what they will "get" when they invite you to their meeting or their party.

You keep your remarks brief and to the point. Your communication is uncomplicated (no, not dumbed down, just uncomplicated). The simplicity of your discourse can offer a breath of fresh air in a world where so many others speak in jargon, euphemism, bet-hedging equivocation or hyper cautious legalese. You call it like you see it, and often you are the one to say what no one else around you will dare to. In the classic fairy tale, you would have been the boy who shouted out "The emperor has no clothes!"

Most admirable of all, you are an authentic individual, true to yourself and to what you believe. Artifice and pretense are not for you. Even people who are put off by your style of communication will never call you hypocritical or two-faced.

But here's the bad news; they are going to call you some other things.

How Direct Speakers Make Others Crazy

Undiplomatic, brusque, rude, oblivious to the feelings of others, shallow and uncompassionate: does this sound like anyone you know? Chances are that as a Direct speaker you do not see yourself this way. As far as you are concerned you are being honest and straightforward. It's true you do not go out of your way to spare anyone's feelings, but at least you're not wasting anyone's time.

The problem is that in spite of your many strengths, there are people who cannot absorb what you say because they are suspect of your motives. Some think you cannot control your impulses. They fear that you are dangerous, a loose cannon who might go off on them at any second. Some just think you are mean.

That said, one of the conundrums about being a Direct speaker is that some of you can get away with it more than others can. If you're, say, a brain surgeon or an airline pilot – a specially skilled professional on whom others' lives may literally depend – you're pretty much allowed to say whatever you want with impunity. In fact, doing so adds to your cachet. If you're an ultra-successful maverick entrepreneur or infallible investment guru, or self-made billionaire in any field, you're never perceived as rude, just colorful. But if you're more of an average mortal, even a very talented one, it would benefit you immeasurably to try to bridge any interpersonal communication gaps you could be suffering.

Direct types generally make outstanding leaders, especially for high-paced organizations. We have found in our experience that many Evolutionaries we have met are Direct communicators. Their approach enables them to cut through the clutter, focus on what's most important, and translate their values into action. But your leadership will be most effective when you step outside of your stream of consciousness for a bit and notice what is going on around you.

Clarifying Strategies for Direct Speakers

For Direct speakers – as well as the other two types of communicators – the most important thing is to simply acknowledge that other worldviews exist and are valid. All the orientations work in different ways, but all must work in concert.

But it's not enough to simply think, "Okay, I know you other folks are out there." As a Direct speaker, the onus falls on you to make certain that your directness is not misinterpreted. Yes, you want your words to be taken at face value, but such is not human nature. Like it or not, others draw inferences from what you say. The quality of their inferential process in detecting and ascribing motive allows them to interpret a critical comment as a personal offense or as a key piece of coaching.

We know what you're thinking: What am I, a mind reader? No, you're not. That's why you need to ask questions. If you've just evaluated someone's work in your usual no-holds barred manner, remember that he or she might not have taken it in the objective spirit in which you genuinely offered it. Ask: Are you okay? Did I upset you? Do you understand why I said what I did and why I need you to do what I asked?

We are not suggesting that you back off from who you are – only that you remember to check in after a conversation. And even more critical – be clear about your motive for your communication right from the beginning. Say, "I am sharing this feedback with you because I believe you have great potential in your work, and I feel you have what it takes to use the feedback I am giving you to achieve excellence." It might sound like "a pain" to have to be more explicit about your motive for giving feedback, but that is not a good excuse for not doing it. Participating in a culture involves a continual trade-off of costs and rewards. It will cost you some time and effort to do the additional communication work, but your reward will be that others will be far more able to take in what you say and act on it in a positive way rather than nurse hurts and grievances that will stand not only in their way but also in yours.

Situational Speakers

What's So Great About Situational Speakers?

We have already mentioned that the three communication orientations exist along a continuum. Picture Direct types at the far left and Bonders at the far right. Situational types are in the middle.

Now picture that each type has a set of building blocks. These blocks form their worldview; from them each type tries to build structures to accommodate every communication situation. As a Situational type you start out with more blocks to work with than do Direct types. You can create more configurations, and so you have more options and more flexibility.

You are good at and dedicated to manifesting just the right "face" at just the right time once you have defined any given situation. At a meeting you'll wear your no-nonsense meeting face; at the after-work bowling alley party you'll wear your affable bowling face (and your bowling shoes because you always know what the rules are and like to follow them).

You rely on and value blocks of structured time that connote a certain social meaning. At work, you are the one that makes sure the Monday morning meeting happens and that everyone has an agenda; at home you are the one who champions the family dinner hour, plans get-togethers with the neighbors and relatives and never forgets a birthday or anniversary.

You are just as organized about thoughts as you are about time – good at framing things and placing them in conceptual buckets so that you and others can make sense of them. Your knack for remembering things has often gotten others out of a jam. (When planning for a camping trip, you're the one who remembers to pack the tent stakes, the flashlight batteries and the compass.)

In short, you are great at "care and feeding." You are a stabilizing force, the glue stick of your workplace. No organization could thrive, or even survive, without you. We have found that fewer Evolutionaries have a Situational communication orientation. It is less suited to the transformational change they so often seek in their careers and their lives.

How Situationals Can Make Others Crazy

Sometimes life is not fair. Sometimes things do not fit into neat categories. And sometimes you have to do things that fall outside of the realm of your official job description in order to accomplish a goal, change an organization or solve a problem. All of this disturbs Situational communicators, and when you are disturbed you dig in your heels about enforcing the rules and roles you hold so dear.

But to Direct types, who just want to move forward, rules or no, and to Bonders, who live to cross even the most well-established boundaries, you are a buzz killer – a card-carrying member of the fun police. As much as these other types may value your skills and reliability when things are running along normally, they will cite you for "driving them to distraction" in any situation that they feel calls for fast change and ad hoc solutions. Let's face it: you are generally not at your best when things are in flux. Rapid change offends your innate sense of order and your affinity for tradition.

Another complaint that is sometimes heard about Situationals is that you are superficial. Your responses can be so situation-driven that Bonders suspect you give the human element short shrift. Although you are the kind of person who can have a heart-felt cry at a stranger's funeral – so caught up are you in the situation and its attendant expectations – others may see such behavior as indicative less of empathy than of rote conformity.

Clarifying Strategies for Situationals

As a Situational, what you do is valuable and important. One of the things you need to do more of is to let people know that – and to remember that yourself. Don't get so caught up in your tasks that you neglect to notice that without you and others like you, your organization would be far more chaotic and inefficient. Your motive is to keep the social structure in place, and you are good at it.

On the other hand, it wouldn't hurt you to lighten up a little bit. Yes, meetings have to happen but they don't have to be as painful as they usually are. Think about helping your colleagues to have better meetings – perhaps ones that allow for a little off-the-agenda banter and brainstorming, or perhaps even ones that take place at the bowling alley between frames.

We are not asking you to morph into another type of person.

But you can be more cognizant of others' motives and try not to take things so personally. Sure, being in the middle of the communication spectrum, you still get some abuse from both sides, but don't let it throw you. Be philosophical about it: "Ah, here comes the abuse, it's right on time." Deep down, remain calm in the knowledge of how much everyone needs you.

Bonding Speakers

What's So Great about Bonding Speakers?

Boy, are you fun to go out to lunch with and to travel with! You are someone who makes friends wherever you go, not to mention your ability to get the bartender to pour you and all your colleagues free shots of tequila whenever you're in the mood.

Charismatic and charming, you are able to find something in common with virtually everyone and begin to forge a relationship based on that commonality. What's more, you believe that business is all about the relationship.

Of all the types, you also have the biggest number of building blocks in your block box. You can structure your communication so that it mirrors the communication of anyone with whom you are trying to make a connection. At the extreme of this orientation, Bonders can identify equally with almost anyone. They like snowboarding; you like snowboarding – or else you would like to like snowboarding and hope they will enlighten you about its many joys along with the particulars of where to do it, when to do it, how to do it and what equipment you will need.

Anything but an elitist, you are an equal opportunity connection-maker. To you, everyone is interesting and anyone is as interesting as the next person. If you've ever watched the show *Dirty Jobs* on the Discovery Channel, you'll spy this trait in the show's host, Mike Rowe. Rowe celebrates unsung heroes who do unthinkable jobs that few of us would want to take on. He profiles everyone from sludge recyclers, hippo keepers and bug breeders, to salt miners, pig farmers and pigeon poop cleaner-uppers. Not afraid to get his own hands dirty in the process, Rowe is genuinely fascinated with each and every job he surveys, and he sincerely values each person who does each job.

As a Bonder, you have time for everyone, or at least you have the heartfelt desire to make time. And when you do spend time with someone you leave them with the impression that at that moment they are the most important person you have ever encountered. This can be highly motivational for those that interact with a Bonding communicator. Many Evolutionaries we have worked with possess this Bonding trait. They know how to connect quickly, establish meaningful relationships as a matter of course, and inspire people to believe not only in an idea, but in their ability to do almost anything!

All in all, you sound like a pretty great human being. So: why on earth do so many people get angry with you so often?

How Bonders Make Others Crazy

For one thing, people can see Bonders as fickle. Sure, they might feel good when they are on the Bonder's radar screen, but they feel betrayed when the Bonder has moved on to bonding with someone else.

Bonders are often pegged with being indecisive as well – or conversely, incredibly decisive as you frequently make snap decisions in the spur of the moment. Because Bonders can find a way to agree with almost everyone, many people come away thinking that they've convinced you that their idea or approach to a given situation is best. But if they listen carefully, they will hear that Bonders are not given to firm commitment. You couch your agreements in what some call weasel-speak: *I think we might be able to…; I think it's important to reach out…; It would be super if we could do that.* Too often all this *faux* agreement just confuses the issue at hand and incites conflict instead of resolving it.

Bonders are also accused of being so busy bonding that you forget you are accountable for deliverables. And it is true that at times Bonders can be more interested in the conversation than the end game. There are a few people in the world whose entire job is solely about bonding. In your dream scenario, Bonders would only have to do lunch – that's it – and it is understood that others will follow through with the details. But most of us in the real world do not enjoy that luxury.

Clarifying Strategies for Bonders

For obvious reasons, we are not suggesting that Bonders surrender their many charms. Your ability to captivate and inspire those around you gives you incredible Evolutionary potential. However, it is important to focus on the end game – outcomes are paramount. Periodically ask: "What am I producing?" and "What is the goal?"

We mentioned before that Bonders have more communication building blocks than any other type. They are a bit like those Eskimos that have 16 words for snow, or like oenophiles who have 183 ways to describe the taste of a wine. But just because you have a lot of blocks does not mean it's a good idea to play with all of the blocks all of the time. Fortunately, you can always downsize to a subset, taking your cues from the Situational or Direct orientation. You do not need to abandon who you are, but keep in mind that there is no shame – and sometimes a lot of merit – in saying to someone, for example, "I love you like a brother, but we have to get this work done."

Before you go too far down the bonding road, check in with yourself and see if you're about to overstep your bounds. If so, consider this piece of Will Rogers' advice: *Never miss a good opportunity to shut up.*

Lay Your Motives on the Table

Now we have been around long enough to know that no matter what communication orientation you fall into, you are not going to instantly take all of our advice – no matter how much you paid for this book. It takes time and practice to "step outside yourself," broaden your range and alter long-entrenched habits. So, while you are working on traversing your own Evolutionary path, we will reinforce just one essential communication lesson to hold onto: When you feel that someone is misunderstanding you or that they are feeling threatened by what you are saying, lay your motive on the table. Whether your motive *is I want to crush the competition* or *I want to beat this deadline* or *I want to follow the rules* or *I want to stop following the rules and have some fun for a change*, just say so. You would be amazed how many problems this will eliminate before they can take root.

Remember, communication is multi-layered:

- There is you and there is me.
- There is your perception of me.
- And then there is my perception of your perception of me.

These three levels drive functional and dysfunctional relationships. If you've been married or in a significant romantic relationship for, say, more than an hour you know how this works. You and your loved one are having a chat. You say something – *innocently enough* – about guessing there's not much food in fridge. They scowl and fold their arms across their chest. They hear you accusing them of not shopping for dinner. You were about to ask them out to dinner but now they seem like they are in such a bad mood for *no reason* that you have second thoughts. You both eat leftovers in silence and go to bed angry.

R.D. Laing called this "the spiral of reciprocating perspectives." At your house you might call it Thursday. But you know what we mean. Think how much grief you could have saved if you'd said, "I'm starved. Want to go to Red Lobster?"

It's not our goal to make psychotherapists of everyone. This is not mumbo-jumbo. Just say what you want and – here's the really important part – *say why you want it*. What are the reasons behind your stated goal? How did you arrive at this decision or preference? Did you reject any other options? What will the decision's impact be? The more clarity you can bring to your motive in every situation the better off everyone is. Evolutionary Communicators are masters of laying their motives on the table. And that's essential for lasting and successful transformational change initiatives.

People evaluate your communication as successful to the extent that they feel they have visibility into your motives and they resonate with those motives. A 2006 study that surveyed roughly 300 managers and employees at over 100 U.S. employers found that employees of companies where decisions were explained more fully were more than twice as likely to support those decisions as workers who got less information. And needless to say, support translates into effort, enthusiasm and accomplishment. Conversely, when people don't know why a new initiative has come down from on high they are apt to resist it. They're not being deliberately uncooperative. They just have nothing to hold onto.

CHAPTER 5

Evolutionary Teams

Evolutionary Wisdom

All you have to do is tune into national news to know that the
Navy SEALs train awesome teams. The SEAL teams do the impossible, make "miracles" happen, defy all odds. With a single mission,
they can change the world. In short, they are the model for what
it means to be truly Evolutionary. Like many curious observers
before us, we asked Captain Steve Ahlberg, "How do you create
Evolutionary Teams?"

*CAPTAIN STEVE AHLBERG: In Basic Underwater Demolition/SEAL (BUD/S)
training, we call the exercises we put people through "evolutions" because
we believe each step of the training process is an evolutionary process. The
evolutions we use work to build what I believe are the best examples of what
a Team really is. We train people at every level: individual, pair, small group
and entire class. For example, in BUD/S you are tested on an individual level
when they tie your hands behind your back, tie your feet together, and
throw you in the swimming pool. You are expected to swim several lengths
of the pool, go to the bottom in the deep end and pick up a diving mask in
your mouth and then continue to bob up and down or tread water until an
instructor tells you to get out. At first when the instructors tell you about the
evolution you think, "Oh this is going to be really hard, I may not be able to
do it, I might have to quit." But then you find out that you can do it – most*

people in the training can do it – and you learn a lot about yourself and what makes you tick and what motivates you. You are also paired with a swim buddy and conduct various evolutions as a pair, such as long swims in the ocean. We put people in pairs to see if they can work with one other person – that is the key to teams – if you can work well with one other person, then you can likely work well in a team. For the longest of our swims, the top half of the class (the first pairs to finish the swim) got hot showers, but for the second half of the class, the hot water would not be available so you got a cold shower. It always "paid to be a winner"! Additionally, it wasn't just a straight swim because there was a huge seaweed bed in the center. The instructors warn you not to try taking a shortcut across it, but people still try and they inevitably get tangled and slowed in the process. The best route is to swim the long way around. You have to stay disciplined as a pair and not try what appears from your perspective in the water to be a shortcut. You want to finish as quickly as possible but you don't want to swim too fast and stress your swim buddy out nor do you want your buddy to swim too fast and feel like you are holding him back. You want to swim together, swim in harmony, and communicate to determine your strategy for the entire swim. This teaches you to really communicate with someone else, how to motivate each other, and finish successfully. In groups of seven people (a boat crew), you are given a small rubber boat to take everywhere with you. You paddle it for miles and you carry it on your heads for miles. The instructors have you paddle out through the surf, flip the boats over, then flip them back, get back in, land it and launch it on boulders, and use the boat as a place to elevate your feet as you do push ups. Every time you do an evolution with the boat incorrectly you have to do it again. The trick is to learn how to stay motivated, work together, and keep communicating effectively and clearly. You start out using a lot of four-letter words! But soon you learn there are better and more meaningful ways to communicate to get the job done. It's in these type of evolutions that you learn how to be a leader, how to communicate, how to plan, how to strategize, how to problem solve, and how to engage in teamwork. As a whole class you go on long runs – up to 16 miles – in formation on the beach in boots and long pants. The goal is to both meet the required time and to stick together as a class. Of course you have people with different levels of running ability so getting the whole class through the run together in formation is a matter of planning, teamwork, communication, strategy, and motivation. You have a team goal to start as a group and end as a group. If you don't finish as a class, you do it all over again. This is where you learn how to help others, how to ask for help when you need it, and how to be receptive to help when it is offered. Before I got to BUD/S, I had taken classes on team building and leadership but nothing was ever this effective.

If you are anything like us, you are probably pretty impressed by that story. But you might also be thinking, "Sure, elite teams like the Navy SEALs can operate like that, but what about us mere mortals trying to wrestle with Excel reports and timesheets? How does this work in business?" We asked that same question, and here's what Captain Ahlberg had to say.

CAPTAIN STEVE AHLBERG: *I have seen experiential training work with banks, construction companies, youth groups, in many places of business. People think they might be the best leader in the world and/or on the organizational chart they are the leader, but in experiential situations they may find that no one is following them. It is usually true back at the office as well. During experiential training you learn a lot about yourself and others. My biggest issue concerning Teams in the business world is that they throw a group of people together and call them a team. The group is not a Team, they are just work groups. These work groups are given a task but they still have their regular job to go back to. Real Teams like great sports Teams or SEAL Platoons – which I think are the best examples of Teams anywhere— are much more than just a group of people. Real Teams are groups of people that have complementary skills, are bonded by shared experiences, and have the common vision of a desired end state—they have a reason for being. Teams collaborate and focus with total commitment to achieving a defined end state. This sounds like a simple definition for Team but it is not easy to build a real Team. One thing making a Team special as compared to a work group is they are allowed the luxury of focus on whatever it is that needs to be done. A work group typically has other distractions such as their regular job. Another problem with Teams in the business environment is they* *are often kept together much too long. Real Teams have a shelf life of maybe 18–24 months. If you have a real Team their work will be intense and they have to stay focused. People can only function at the highest level for so long before they need some downtime. Even professional sports Teams don't play twelve months a year—they have several months between seasons.*

Real Teams can be built in business. A Team can be built in any environment if they are allowed the luxury of focus, time for meaningful collaboration, and receive experiential training that bonds them together. You need training that is meaningful where key lessons can be learned – what we call an "evolution." One of the things that makes Navy SEAL Teams special is the kind of instruction and training they go through in terms of being collaborative and experiential. By collaborative I mean really working together to solve one problem after another in situations they have never faced before. The training is meaningful and focused on teamwork. Creating elite Teams is done through collaborative experiential training that gets more and more challenging. Instructors present one challenge after another to a swim pair or to a boat crew, or class, and trainees have to figure out how to resolve that challenge and get through it every time. Then, when you make it into an operational SEAL platoon you have a set methodology for meeting new challenges and are not intimidated by them. Instructors keep ratcheting up the pressure all through training. You can use the same principles to Train teams in the workplace. What that does in the end is work to create a Team bond that is just unbelievable. When we do this kind of training over and over in the SEALs we get to know each other so well that at night when you see the shadow of one of your platoon teammates you can usually tell what he is thinking just by how he moves. If you do enough Team building, even in the business world, you will learn a lot about each other, your character, the character of others, how you work, how you think, how to best communicate, how to plan, how to problem solve together, and what the capabilities of each person on your Team is. You will not be intimidated by seemingly impossible situations.

Of course, Evolutionary Teams are created through more than just great training. First you have to have the right people for the team. And that means a rigorous recruitment and hiring process, where organizations are willing to invest the time and resources to get it right the first time! Geoff Gilmore shares how they approach hiring talent at Climax to ensure elite teams of engineers that solve some of the toughest problems in innovative design.

GEOFF GILMORE: *We are clear about who we are at Climax and what we are trying to accomplish. We get this message out through traditional marketing, social media, and word of mouth, and we are explicit about it in our interview process. We have a rigorous interview process because we want to make sure that we are the right company for the people we hire just as much as they are the right person for the company. Each candidate that we are considering has the chance to meet with over 10 members of the management team and other people in the company. Why would we want to unintentionally mislead someone when it comes to who the people are at Climax, what the culture is like, and our values? We are much more successful and profitable when people are thrilled with their decision to work at Climax. That's why we spend time to learn about each person's passion – what really motivates them about their work and what they like to do. We look for people who have hobbies that align with their work. We want your home life to make you stronger at work and your work life to make you stronger at home. We invest a lot of time in the interview process, making it as inclusive as possible. It takes longer, but it's worth it. Not to just avoid the cost of a mis-hire but much more importantly to have the power of an engaged and committed workforce.*

We had the opportunity to tour Climax, and while the custom solution tools they produce are nothing short of impressive, we were just as blown away by their unique approach to celebrating success. Captain Ahlberg tells us that experiential training bonds teams. But we saw first-hand that celebrating everyday wins is also powerful glue for binding people around shared goals and strategy.

GEOFF GILMORE: *In many organizations you see a tension between the sales teams and the production teams. We simply don't engage in that type of politics at Climax. We gave a tour recently and during the visit one of our* *sales team members called out over the loud speakers that he just closed a deal for over $200K. The employees in all of our teams cheered in response. And then it's right back to work so we can deliver that order on-quality, on-time for our customer. We announce every sale right when it is closed, for the whole company to hear it. Why do we do that? So that everyone can celebrate the sale together. These collective celebrations are powerful – not just for morale, but in connecting the dots that we are all in this together, that we are all on the same team. How many production teams do you know that hear and celebrate a sale the moment it happens? It's to unify our purpose. So we celebrate together as a whole.*

We think that's pretty cool. The practice of real time shared celebration at Climax is a great example of a low-cost, high-return practice that makes a huge difference for team morale and works to keep shared organizational goals front and center in day-to-day operations where so often the bigger strategic picture is lost. We are willing to bet that simple solutions like this concept of shared celebrations are possible in most organizations, but are rarely explored. Ask yourself what sort of small gestures you could add to your organization's way of working that might pay big dividends for bonding teams together or motivating employees to work across departments?

Why You Need Evolutionary Teams

Evolutionary Teams are more likely to execute on the organization's strategic objectives because they demand clarity of mission and the sense that it's important. The Evolutionary Team ideally exists with one foot in the traditional "business-as-usual" culture of the organization and one foot in the world of innovation, change and new possibilities. These teams should also enjoy a Charter that completely frees them to be innovative outside of the "business as usual" if your company is ready to take that leap. Evolutionary Teams are truly at their best when the organization is in crisis mode and true revolutionary action is critical for survival. But we find that most organizations are looking for change that is a little less dramatic. And that sort of smaller, but significant strategic shift in an organization is also where Evolutionary Teams excel. Whatever the change on the horizon, what makes Evolutionary Teams special is their transformative potential. Because they have the ability to balance between organizational traditions and pioneering vision, Evolutionary Teams can do what other teams can't: they can raise the bar for what is possible in your organization, your industry, and even the world.

You need Evolutionary team members because even if the team fails, you will know more and be better off than working with non-Evolutionary team members. With ordinary team members, giving up is an option. Failing because of team dynamics is an option. Failing because ideas were not vetted well is an option. The team may fail, and you won't necessarily know why. But when you have Evolutionary team members, even in failure you will have an understanding of how and why that failure happened – and this knowledge will give you confidence in the endeavor. Even if you lose the game, you are assured to know much more about the opponent than you did before.

Pitfalls. The downside to Evolutionary team members is that they do need to be reined in sometimes. Working with an Evolutionary can sometimes feel as one client of ours says, "Like trying to boil the ocean." At some point Evolutionaries will push too far, think too big – it is in their nature to pursue excellence and shoot for the moon. This will not always be practical. But it will be a force that pushes your teams harder and creates the kind of culture where winning as a team is more likely.

How Evolutionaries Work in Teams

Let's get one thing straight – Evolutionaries *love* to be on teams! Sure, Evolutionaries like "rah rah" and relational development, but the driving motivation is to get things done, facilitate meaningful change, and bring about desired results through the work of the team. They are inherently outcome oriented. They are willing to engage in efforts that are research-based, process-based or relational-based depending on what is necessary to forward a desired outcome. They will not be happy with "fluffy" interactions for the sake of it. But they will be the first to suggest soft skills training if that's what it takes to better bond the team, to increase morale to get the job done.

This also means that the Evolutionary is constantly thinking of the competencies they need to develop to be better members of their teams. That might be learning how to operate a complex piece of machinery or software program. Or it might be to be learning how to order Chinese food in Beijing on the next team business trip. The point is that gaining "badges" in the skills that forward the team toward its goals is seen as a worthy pursuit.

Evolutionary Team Members:
- *Align to the mission of the team*
- *Take pride in being a team member*
- *Have humility around weaknesses*
- *Are supremely confident in their strengths*

Evolutionaries cannot participate where they are not **aligned to the mission of the team.** In just a moment we're going to tell you that humility is an essential Evolutionary characteristic. But for now, we are going to make the observation that a project team's Charter should be audacious – seemingly outrageous. There should be a level of pressure, urgency, importance, criticality, difficulty, that all add up to the inescapable conclusion that there is no way that any individual alone can solve the problem or accomplish the goal and there is no way the organization could solve the problem or accomplish the goal in its normal working patterns. If you create a team to do something that is fundamentally easy or inconsequential or achievable through the normal workings of the organization, then you have woefully damaged the individuals and you have weakened your organization. It is not neutral – from the Evolutionary's point of view, it is much worse to have a team doing something that is not incredibly cool than to do nothing at all. So, the ability to establish your Evolutionary Team on a "burning platform" will do two things: 1) provide the team the focus they need to accomplish an extraordinary goal, and 2) not make that platform part of your ongoing organization. The bottom line here is that you *must make the project important*. If Evolutionary team members don't feel there is a strong shared value, they will make one up. They simply function from a place where working for something bigger than themselves is always a critical motivator.

Evolutionaries believe that to be a good team player is one of the best characteristics that any human can have. For this reason alone, the Evolutionary **is proud of his or her identity as a team member.** Being a good team member is a personal value for the Evolutionary that is *independent* of any organizational goal or project outcome. This Evolutionary characteristic connects back to our discussion of social identity in leadership. If you can imagine sliding down a fire pole, throwing your gear on, hopping in the truck and then finding yourself in an intense battle against a raging fire, knowing you have to depend on the people around you for your life, then of course you are going to take deep pride in wearing the badge of your team. The emotional trappings of the team become paramount in the way you define who you are. The mistake people tend to make is to say: "Well, let's get our team some shirts." But the magic is not in the shirt, it is in *fighting the fire together*. It is the pride that comes from participating in something bigger than any one person. Evolutionaries understand that shared excellence and failure are how you foster strong team loyalty.

Evolutionary team members **have a sense of humility around their weaknesses.** They are thrilled to be dependent on the talents of other team members in order to accomplish a mission (think of great sports teams). This is not about saying: "Well, Bob is a better numbers person so he should do this task." It's about interlocking strength with support to achieve team end goals. A common mistake people make is to simply divide tasks on a team up by individual skill sets. But what they should be doing is looking for what they can do together by *combining* different skill sets and leveraging the bonding power inherent in partnerships. It is subtle, but important – it's not about stepping back out of humility, but about stepping in and engaging in a way that puts you second to the higher goals of the partner you are bound to and the team. Remember the lesson we learn from the Navy SEALs about the power of working in pairs. Evolutionary team members are going to work exponentially better with a "swim buddy." There is also humility in the learning process associated with recognizing and improving on managing weaknesses as well. If you have to stand on the sidelines for a time to just observe what is happening, then you are still responsible for being an active member of the debrief to share your observations, ideas and opinions. Your point of view is always valuable. You are always a member of the team, whether your skill set is being featured or not.

Evolutionaries are also **supremely confident in their strengths and what they bring to the team.** And this is about bringing the whole game of the team up – bringing these skills to the team raises the bar of the whole team as a collective force. But this is not about being a hero. Evolutionary teams often produce heroes (like SEAL missions) but achieving hero status is not what drives the team. So, just because you are great at designing PowerPoint slides, you should not end up doing the whole project. You have the responsibility to find ways to connect with the opportunities for support, feedback and point of view that come from the other members of the team. And if you know something best and you are not teaching others, then the only conceivable excuse for that from an Evolutionary point of view is that it is not the right time to teach. If you are doing an emergency landing on an airplane, and you are the only one who can land it, it is not a good time to do a seminar on how to land an airplane. But it is your obligation to find a way to teach that skill to others once that plane is landed. That is what it means to be an Evolutionary team member.

Forming an Evolutionary Team

The secret recipe:

Step 1: Prepare the culture for teamwork. You do this by making short-term, highly manageable assignments to pairs of people. Just as Captain Ahlberg tells us that "if you can't work with one other person, you can't work with a team," you first have to socialize your people to sharing work and sharing accountability. This does not come naturally to most people! Captain Ahlberg tells us that it is three-part cycle, there's the planning piece, then there is the operation and then there is the debrief piece, to create the complete ecosystem for any kind of shared work. You need to teach this to your teams, and hold them accountable to it. This philosophy has to become a part of how all work gets done in the organization. People always ask us for examples. Here's an example:

> You are looking into adding social media as a part of a new networking piece. You assign two people to this task – one from marketing and one from IT to write a short three- to five-page brief on the classic mistakes that other businesses have made in using social media. They are asked to present their findings in writing and to present them in person at the next management team meeting. Their performance is evaluated in a follow-up meeting with open discussion about what they did well and where they can improve, and they are thanked for their efforts. Meanwhile a dozen other such assignments are given out to other work pairs. At first this will seem odd, but within six months you will have the foundational base you need for a highly effective, motivated Evolutionary Team cul-

ture. Within three months you can begin asking teams of four and six to do the same thing on a larger scale.

Step 2: Create a Charter for the larger cross-functional team that clearly defines the strategic objective this team will be responsible for executing. In a perfect world, people would volunteer and apply to be on the team and would be tested or auditioned for the team. The participants would both volunteer for and earn their right to be on the team. That's in a perfect world. We know that cannot always happen.

Step 3: Form the team. There are hundreds of books dedicated just to this topic alone – project teams. There are also hundreds of processes for forming project teams. We recommend you read them and choose a process best for your organization. But, to get you started, here are some of our most basic guidelines for selecting team members and forming an Evolutionary Team:

- Don't choose all managers or supervisors (this is a classic mistake).
- Have at least three departments represented on the team.
- Limit the size of the team to the size of the work. The best teams are five to fifteen people.
- Unless you are going to fundamentally change a person's job to be solely the work of the team, ask people to serve for only 90 days at a time.
- Give the team space and time to work on the project.
- Team members should end each meeting establishing clarity for what needs to be done and how the team will communicate those ongoing efforts with the rest of the organization. Like all good teams they will speak with "one voice."
- The team should make progress presentations to senior leaders on a regular basis.
- The team should have a team sponsor that is a senior leader in the organization, and a team leader.

Step 4: Identify milestones and key performance indicators that the team will use to measure progress and develop a project plan.

Step 5: End the project on a fixed calendar date. If the goal has not been accomplished another team must be ready to take over and the first team will need to account for their failure.

The team becomes Evolutionary when a strategic organizational goal is accomplished and transformational change occurs, but it's so seamless that no one really knows how it happened or whom to thank. Much like the SEAL teams, success often means that the bomb did not go off, the hostage came home or the evil dictator is dead. The outcome is what is noticed, but the team is in the background. The Evolutionary team *chooses* to go to the moon and getting there is the reward. The whole world benefited from the science these remarkable NASA teams created, but no one remembers their names.

> ### Special Note
>
> Captain Ahlberg warns us that most projects in organizations are executed by "work groups" that we mistakenly call teams. Teams are much more than work groups. We believe that work groups become truly Evolutionary when they transform into real teams. So, you must give the group you choose permission to become a **team.** This means they need the special training, time, and resources to develop a culture *in and of themselves*. That's why you also must let the team stand down at the end date. Where work groups can go on and on, teams need to have an end – just as great sports teams have a "season" and a down time, so do your elite Evolutionary teams need to have a cycle of life.

CHAPTER 6

Evolutionary Innovation

Evolutionary Wisdom

Innovation. It's buzz word number one in business today. Everyone wants it. But it remains mysterious and elusive. It is the rare company indeed that can consistently innovate and transform. But Oregon Iron Works and United Streetcar are ahead of the curve when it comes to achieving consistent and profitable innovation. And driving this unique innovative culture is Chandra Brown. That's just one reason President Obama has asked her to serve on his jobs council to define the future of manufacturing jobs in the United States.

CHANDRA BROWN: We are constantly reinvesting in innovation. We take the money from our sales and we put it back into the equipment, into the tooling, into the machines, and of course into the fundamental base for innovation – our workforce. Oregon Iron Works is about using our core competencies to adapt to an ever-changing environment. We started this company building a wide variety of products, from hydroelectric projects, to bridges, to boats. We have built hundreds of boats in the past few decades and we have learned that the marine environment is incredibly harsh. It takes serious expertise to work successfully with "metal and water." We have become experts on that environment. So we started asking ourselves "What's going to be happening in the future in the marine environment? How can we apply our expertise to future trends?" So now Oregon Iron Works is the first company on the West Coast to build a wave energy buoy off the coast of Oregon to generate energy from the waves. It's a simple idea – metal in water – but we know a lot about how to make that work. We can take the special skill sets from a traditional boat building industry and bring them forward to potentially build wave energy devices, which are a clear growth industry for the future.

Another example is United Streetcar. This is a project I worked on from the beginning, from the idea that we would begin building streetcars. And to see the unveiling of the first American-made streetcar in 58 years is a fantastic story to be a part of. We have been a part of the creation of a new industry in the United States. There are over 65 cities in the United States looking at streetcars not only for the transit purposes but also for the economic development, the green benefit of an electric vehicle, and the density that can go along a streetcar line which has huge revitalization benefits beyond just moving people from point A to point B. Innovation for us is about looking at the needs of the future and adapting our current expertise to the new needs.

Chandra shows us that Evolutionary Innovation is not about changing who you are, or abandoning your core skill sets – it's about maximizing your strengths by applying them to new challenges, problems and opportunities. And while one huge part of innovation is adapting existing skills to new applications, just as important is envisioning those new applications. In short, how do Evolutionaries get new ideas?

CHANDRA BROWN: *I often get asked if I have a crystal ball. Why did you think that streetcars would be an emerging market? Why would you look at wave energy? How do you know what is the next big thing? It's an incredibly difficult question to answer because there is no formula or specific science. I am a big believer in taking in great amounts of data from as wide a variety of sources as possible. So I read a ton, books – fiction and non-fiction – lots of different papers, trade magazines, poetry, biographies, everything. I serve on over seven non-profit boards including some for the State of Oregon, and all are very diverse. I am on the Oregon Innovation Council so we are circulating* *new ideas all the time. I travel a lot. I like to see what other countries are doing, and how they do it – this is incredibly beneficial. The first-hand knowledge of actually seeing something being built – the process versus just reading about it – is the best inspiration. Finding the next big thing is really about synthesizing a lot of different data input. I know what my company's skills and strengths are and so it's about making that leap in how to apply them to the next thing coming along. A lot of the battle is to actually be aware that you need to continually be changing and improving. You have to have an embracing, entrepreneurial attitude for new things to pop. And once people know you are open to ideas, they will begin to bring them to you more often. A lot of idea people now come to me and say, "Hey Chandra, can you do a prototype of this new product X that we think is the wave of the future?" It's priceless to be in a place where people will come to you with new ideas. I see my role as always being open and available to take that call – pretty much anyone can call me with an idea and I will listen to them – most of them probably won't work and are outlandish and outrageous and would never be anything we would be interested in but I still find value in listening. I may agree with them or I may disagree with them, but either way the conversation helps frame the constant data input to keep working on synthesizing and predicting where emerging markets will be.*

If you are anything like us, at this point you are probably thinking, "Sure, but if you take in every idea that comes your way and you commit to prototyping even a small fraction of those ideas, you are making a huge investment. What happens when it doesn't pan out?"

CHANDRA BROWN: *At Oregon Iron Works and United Streetcar there of course have been failures. I think the most important thing is to take the lessons learned and to treat all failures as investments. So often for us a failure in one area will lead to success in a different area. For example, building bridges has always been a baseline skill for us. But we build other things too. Yet, we compete against companies that only build bridges, so of course they have incredible expertise in bridge building. They have an advantage because they are not also building boats and streetcars and all of these* *other fantastic "distractions." So we made the decision that we will no longer compete in doing incredibly simple bridges. Instead, we focus on highly technical bridges that need to survive earthquakes and that have incredibly high standards. We learned that when we weren't being competitive it was because we weren't taking advantage of our diversity – because we can take lessons learned from one industry and apply them to another. We can look like geniuses when we take something that we know from aerospace that is more advanced than marine science and we take an aerospace solution and apply it to a marine project. It is really nothing revolutionary, but because those industries don't talk, they don't have that diverse pool of skills and talents that we bring to the table.*

When people think of companies that exemplify innovation, Apple often comes to mind first. But it is the lesser-known companies across the nation like Oregon Iron Works and United Streetcar that drive the American economy, define our identity as a people with pioneering spirit, and provide jobs that challenge people and give them a sense of pride in what they do. In this way, innovation is not just a good business practice, it's our way of life. The story of Oregon Iron Works and United Streetcar reminds us of the power of diversity, and our incredible capacity to be Evolutionary.

We think of Apple when we think of innovation, not just because they are an incredibly agile and creative company, but because technology in general is an innovation-dependent industry. Bluetooth SIG has changed the world forever as the advancement of wireless services is making life easier and more products accessible to people around the world. We asked Mike Foley to share his strategy for staying ahead of an industry where innovation is not just a hot business buzz word, but a way of life.

MIKE FOLEY: *You need to be constantly plugged in with your ear to the ground. And, you have to be out there talking to developers and partners that might fall outside of your current target demographic. If we stuck only to our target demographic we would focus 99% on the mobile phone and what is good for that industry. But if that is all we do, we will miss something,* *we are underutilizing our potential. I want to see another market come out that is as big as the mobile phone, but to see that you have to talk to people outside of the mobile phone industry. I actually think that there are a lot of opportunities right now if we are willing to be a little bit aggressive and willing to take some chances and invest a little bit now for what could be large gains.*

Like Chandra, Mike knows that value of soliciting lots of input, opinions, ideas, and criticisms. And that's the real essence of the Evolutionary Innovator – a strong appetite for gathering a wide variety of information from a wide variety of sources. And at the source of all of this information gathering is Bluetooth SIG's commitment to the consumer experience. Mike knows that the consumer ultimately "governs" these interactions and partnerships he seeks. So, we learn that the Evolutionary Innovator sees his or her job as one of constantly working to gain and refine "perspective." It is about having a perspective on the whole industry, managing the perspectives of all your different membership bases, stakeholders and your internal employees. It is not just about doing your job right; Evolutionary Innovators believe it's really about raising the bar on what the whole potential of what your business is and what it can be.

Why You Need Evolutionary Innovators

Most businesses fail at innovation because of a misguided effort to preserve their legacy. It's not that organizational commitment to building a strong legacy is a bad thing – in fact it is essential to preserve institutional knowledge and culture. But when we become too focused on preserving legacy at the expense of exploring new ideas and taking calculated risks, we pay the price in loss of innovation. You need Evolutionary Innovators to help you look forward. Innovation is about looking forward but not at the expense of your past. And because it is a part of the Evolutionaries' nature to attach themselves to organizations with a culture and mission they believe in, the Evolutionary Innovator will guide your vision toward innovation while honoring the legacy that exists. It may sound simple, but in practice balancing with one foot in legacy and one foot in innovation is a rare ability for most executives. Chandra shows how an Evolutionary Innovator can lead a small company to expand to national and then international success through the consistent search for new opportunities to apply an established set of workforce skills. She explains that, "A lot of leaders I know would resist moving from the concept that 'we build boats, we are a boat company' to 'let's make wave generators.' But you have to be able to say, 'We are going to take a risk, we have to innovate,' and then of course accept that we are also then going to take a chance on failing." If your company needs to transform – if innovation is what you need – then you need leaders like Chandra. You need an Evolutionary.

How Evolutionaries Innovate

We learn from Chandra's story that in innovation and evolution, there will always be missteps along the way. Things don't always work out as planned. But Evolutionary leaders are willing to place bets when it counts and have confidence in themselves and their teams. Sure, sometimes you will invest a significant amount of time and resources into trying a new line of business and it will be a failure. And that failure will often be public. But Evolutionary Innovators know how to look beyond failure for the opportunity on the horizon. They learn from mistakes and apply those lessons to new endeavors. They don't give up, they know how to overcome failure and they don't let fear of the unknown keep them from trying new things, prototyping possibilities, and pushing the envelope ever further.

Evolutionary Innovators:
- **Cast a wide net**
- **Are known as prototypers**

- Are willing to be uncomfortable
- Take a leap of faith

Chandra tells us that when it comes to predicting future trends and making business decisions that are gutsy and often profitable, she **casts a wide net** for information. She explores avenues of data, conversation, and experience that most leaders would never dream of doing. Chandra is not just reading *Iron Worker Weekly* (we don't know if that is a real magazine, but if it is we are sure she reads it!). Her story teaches us that leaders have an obligation to be fully engaged with a whole range of ideas, people and subjects. We deal with executives all the time in our consulting work, and while they are experts in their industries, they are also unbelievably myopic in their leadership. They often feel like if they are not reading something about their specific business then they are not doing their job. Chandra's success is found in her ability to cast her net well beyond her own industry for new ideas and strategies that put her and her companies one step ahead of the competition.

So, Evolutionary Innovation is fundamentally about how widely you cast your net. The more you read, the more people you talk with, the more industries you study, the more you take in, the more likely you are to get the next great idea. Seeking out this wide variety of information comes naturally to Evolutionaries, especially Bonding Evolutionary Communicators as they are already interested in everyone they meet and every experience they encounter. Evolutionaries naturally possess a healthy curiosity, so casting the net and "catching butterflies" is just a way of life for them.

Evolutionary Innovators are also **known as prototypers**. There is a "word on the street" that you can bring them new ideas and they will give you their ear. They ensure that they will always be the first to hear the next great idea by committing themselves to listening to hundreds of not-so-great ideas. Evolutionary Innovators know that it is impossible for them to be the source of all the good ideas, so they build a reputation for being willing to prototype things for others. They market themselves as "doers" and that invites ideas in. Maybe one in a thousand is great, but ensuring that you see hundreds of ideas gives you the best chance of receiving that one great one.

The good news is that prototyping doesn't have to break the bank for your organization. You can build a culture of rapid prototyping simply by lowering the bar on what it means to "give something a try." We are big fans of the book *The Ten Faces of Innovation* by Tom Kelley. In his chapter on prototyping Kelley explains that you can prototype just about everything, as long as you are willing to "not be precious about it." Kelley argues that even the most crude prototypes can predict a successful idea, and the job of organizational leaders is to create an environment where such less-polished prototypes are encouraged. "The best organizations are those that make it culturally acceptable to show off ideas at their rough, early stages because those are the organizations that see a whole lot more ideas."

Perhaps the most difficult requirement for an Evolutionary Innovator is that they *are willing to be uncomfortable.* Just think about it – if you are going to cast your net as widely as possible, your level of tolerance for discomfort must be equally up to the task. You will need to be around people who are much different from you, travel to places that are out of your comfort zone, attend events that you "don't like" (such as NASCAR, or the opera – OK maybe that's just us). In order to bond with new friends you will have to try food that scares you (that sea urchin sushi you think is weird). You will have to constantly push yourself to experience the new and foreign to keep your mind sharp and alive and to remember what it means to do something for the first time. Evolutionary Innovators regularly challenge their biases in life, because they know that this will train them to be more agile and open to innovative opportunities when they arise.

Finally, Evolutionary Innovators are *willing to take leaps of faith.* There is a time and place in great rock climbing where you

Evolutionary Innovation in the Modern World

Evolutionary Innovators are constantly playing at the edges of spheres where the game can be changed. Technology, science, medicine. They will gravitate to places where revolutionary innovations have the most chance to transform the world and the way we live, work and build communities. Sure, you could revolutionize accounting principles, but it is unlikely to change the world as we know it. So you will likely find fewer Evolutionaries pursuing degrees in accounting than in digital advertising or foreign policy. And Evolutionaries are often particularly enthralled with technology. They are often accused of chasing "shiny" things – new trends, fads, and games. They are known as early adopters (and sometimes also as early discarders when the next shiny object comes along). But there has to be a little bit of "geek" in every evolutionary. You don't have to be "in" these industries, but you do have to be attracted to these areas in a way that people might perceive as "nerdiness."

have to let go of your hand- and footholds at the same time to get to the next place. It's called the "dynamic move" and it is so dramatic that it feels crazy. But it is the only way to move forward and make progress. You don't actually have to take the risk – but it is the only way you can get to the top. Evolutionary Innovators are willing to take risks to achieve progress – to evolve. They make big bets. But just like the climber, they will do everything possible to prepare for that bold move and plan for making it.

And this leap of faith is not just something that happens at the beginning of the transformational change in an organization. Evolutionary Innovators know that as the change efforts around implementing innovation progress, faith will be tested again. This is because for most big efforts, the organization and its people are making a substantial investment of time, money, resources, and opportunity cost. Over time, leaders expect the cost to go down, and ROI (real tangible results) to go up. But there is a time in all such efforts where we find that we have made the investment and there are no real results. This is when all the doubt emerges about why/how we made the original investment in the first place. Even true Evolutionary believers begin to doubt; "did we get the right vendor?" "Are we making the right assumptions?" "What if we are wrong?" We call this progression the Zone of Doubt and Blame.

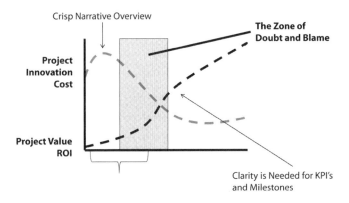

Welcome to the Zone

Evolutionary Innovators are prepared for this Zone – they know it will happen and they know it will take another leap of faith to push through it. But that is the trick – to push through the zone. The key is being able to be bone-level clear about what you are doing and why you are doing it and repeat that message again and again through the zone.

Evolutionary Guidance

By now it should be very clear that Evolutionaries are always going to be found at the center of high-change dynamic situations. And in modern business, that often looks and feels like chaos. You don't need to look far to find the culprit for the chaos. The vast majority of the time you need only look to the integrity (or lack of integrity) in the planning process. Confusion and chaos are rooted in the inability to realize that planning, execution and assessment are iterative not linear. The role of an Evolutionary in a high-change situation is to act as a shock absorber to all of the incidental actions that could throw your plan off course. We observe that people will identify themselves as either "planners" or "doers." The Evolutionary Guide has the unique ability to plan while doing – to reflect and adjust while also in action. The pace of digital business does not tolerate inflexible and static plans. So, Evolutionary Guides are a welcome resource to lead a developmental strategic conversation that may be made up of all kinds of plans and sub-plans.

In this chapter we explore the potential of the Evolutionary Guide. Our experience confirms that organizations that are experiencing high rates of change often show lots of symptoms of stress and dysfunction. Some organizations however seem to be able to exist in a constant state of change and thrive. What's the difference? In a word, the difference is vision. Vision is generally the domain of Senior Leadership and the Board of Directors. The first defining characteristic of Evolutionary Guides is that they get the vision. So when we talk about Evolutionary Guides, we are necessarily talking about your organization's vision and the planning process you use to make your vision real. This is a great chapter for Boards but it is also relevant for anyone who has ever tried to develop, write, socialize or execute a plan. If vision is an essential element in the big picture, guidance is the essential element in realizing that vision. Every plan needs a guide.

We spend a lot of time with Boards, and we spend a lot of time thinking about the concept of guidance. Guidance in its broadest definition is everything from advice and counsel to education and psychological support. The best guides, whether leading a whitewater rapids rafting trip, a climb up Mount Kilimanjaro, or a vision quest, are those that do not just guide the course, but the *conduct* expected while traveling that course. Those are the guides that do more than get us from point A to point B, they change us for the better along the way.

Evolutionary Wisdom

The first thing Evolutionary Guides do is include everyone in the planning process.

CAPTAIN STEVE AHLBERG: The best planners are those who are willing to involve everybody that is going to be a player in the actual execution of the plan. Give a team a mission and let them develop the plan as to how to complete the mission. As the leader, you can always review the plan and say, "Well what if this happened, what if that happened, did you think of this and did you think of that?" Good leadership is about assigning a clear mission and offering only minor guidance to the Team in planning the execution strategy. You can always step in with more guidance later if necessary, but make suggestions and let changes be their idea. In other words, you don't want to present a plan to a Team and expect them to buy it and to execute it. They need to develop it to own it. At the mission planning level of the Team expected to carry out the operation you achieve buy-in by dividing up portions of the execution plan and tasking each person involved to help create a part of it. Then the Team can come together to finalize the entire plan and "buy-in" is achieved. As the leader, you are responsible to keep people focused and on track. By involving the entire Team in the planning you are also able to hear a lot of different ideas that you never would have thought of on your own. These ideas might at first seem totally out of the box but in the end might be the best ideas. Let your ego get out of the way so you, as a leader, can be open to new ideas.

Now, we are not saying that you need to invite every employee into your next planning session! But Evolutionary Guides are always thinking about new and creative ways to plan that allow the people of the organization to "put their fingerprints" on the plan. Sometimes this looks like creating a higher level plan and assigning "sub-plans" to elite teams within the organization to work on for execution strategies. Sometimes it looks like employee surveys and focus groups prior to the planning process. Whatever approach you choose, the key is to be as inclusive as possible.

Why You Need an Evolutionary Guide

We have never said that everyone in an organization needs to be an Evolutionary. We have never said all leaders need to be Evolutionaries. If bold development and transformation are not part of your company vision, then you are really making a mistake in filling your company, and especially your Board of Directors, with Evolutionaries.

Evolutionary Guides are the "stewards of the strategy" for the organization.

There is really nothing more "medieval" or arcane than a Board of Directors. But on another level it is really a classic and powerful idea because the potential of a Board is profound – as we know the power of good groups to accomplish good things. And often what we see is that the Board is one of the potential choke points in an organization's ability to really reach its potential. It may be that the Board can be too conservative or too demanding or too aggressive. But the pivotal point here is that the Board is not a neutral party in driving the strategy and the success of Evolutionaries throughout the organization.

So what is the key element of a Board that will be Evolutionary-friendly as opposed to the Board that will choke the Evolutionary potential of a company? The answer is the time horizon of the strategic vision. We believe that Boards become truly Evolutionary when they begin looking out a long way – 10 to 20 years or, in some rare cases, even longer. And the more the Board can define that environment long term, the better Evolutionaries driving long-term change in the organization can be successful.

Evolutionary Boards offer the kind of guidance that constantly identifies and describes the transformative goal and can stay focused on it over years. They are willing to apply resources to it over years, and hold Evolutionary leaders accountable to it over years. And they are confident enough in this vision and its possibility that they are trusted by the organization to operate in the guidance role. Great guidance garners trust. And when organizations trust their Board, amazing things begin to happen.

But we must warn you – if you have an Evolutionary leader on your Board, this person will likely drive the group crazy! They will always be pushing out to the edge of what is possible. And this may not always be the right course.

Boards that are Evolutionary must commit to bold but long-term visions for long periods of time, and individual Evolutionary members may not have the discipline that the collective needs. It's in the individual Evolutionary leader's nature to go ranging for new paths. You are glad they have these awesome skills, but they should not always be put to use. Just as we want to have an airline pilot that is capable of doing all sorts of skills maneuvers and impressive feats, we don't want them to do those maneuvers when we are on a plane with our family heading to Hawaii for vacation. Just because you are capable of doing something does not mean your job is to do it all the time. You may want Evolutionary leaders guiding your vision precisely because they can adapt and excel in disruptive times, but once a vision is established, pressing for change is not appropriate. At some point, guidance is about establishing a vision – and it can be an audacious vision – and sticking to that vision over the long term, even when it loses its luster and becomes boring to the Evolutionary Guides that first envisioned it.

How Evolutionaries Guide

Chandra Brown tells us "there is no formula for good guidance, you are making a reasoned judgment as a human being and so often we shirk that in lieu of trying to create a system for decisions." This pinpoints the tension in any business that is trying to grow and innovate while also maintaining quality and consistency. We see Boards do this all the time. In an attempt to scale and grow what the organization does well, they mandate that management design and impose "cookie-cutter" processes like job descriptions, technical procedures, and a myriad of systems that are fundamentally designed to remove judgment from the equation in any given situation. And this goal extends to the Board themselves as they begin to write more and more policies designed to remove all judgment from even the highest level of operating the strategy. But, at its heart, guidance is all about judgment.

Evolutionary Boards understand that the function of a truly great strategy is to push guidance down through the organization as a universal competency. The strategy serves as the guide – it provides a lens through which good judgment can be made, without constraining it with too many pre-defined decisioning mechanisms.

Evolutionary Guides:
- *Bring calm to chaos*
- *Know their own minds*
- *Are masters of subtle course correction*
- *Have no predetermined definition of success*

Plans are designed. The team begins execution – excited about the goals ahead. And then the wheels come off the plan (and most likely there is a point where they will). It's in these times that your organization's Evolutionary Guides step in to **bring calm to chaos.** Your organization is better prepared to adapt and flex the plan to meet those changes, because those executing the plan know the plan well – and they also know how to plan well, because you have educated them through the process. And Evolutionary Guides have faith in the team to respond to new scenarios and are able to remain calm.

CAPTAIN STEVE AHLBERG: *Once the execution phase of the plan begins things usually change, and the plan needs to change too. Be flexible and try not to overreact. If the planning phase was done well potential changes have been considered. This is the importance of everyone being involved in the planning and totally familiar with it. Everyone on the* Team *is prepared and can step in and take the lead at any time.*

Evolutionary Guides are able to remain calm and confident in their decisions, even when those decisions are tested, because they **know their own minds.** They are "centered" – they know who they are and what they are about in this world. (This is not to say that they aren't aware of external inputs and are insensitive to the feelings and opinions of those around them, and it is not to say that they know everything or have all the answers, but instead that they have a deep understanding of who they are and it is this confidence that allows them to effectively guide others.) Imagine a snorkeling expedition where a group of tourists sets out with a seasoned local guide to explore the aquatic world. The ocean is a big and mysterious place, as full of danger as it is of wonders. So, even if you are Michael Phelps, you are going to be wearing a life vest. This journey requires more than just expertise, skill and knowledge – the ocean is a complex and nuanced, ever-shifting environment and the guide is there to speak to how to "be" in that world. Again, it's something beyond advice; it's a matter of conduct. It's that ability to be "of the ocean" that makes him or her the *trusted guide* that people follow. Evolutionary Guides have to have more than just expertise, skill and knowledge. They need to be "of the environment" at hand to really guide the organization in it. They must have supreme confidence and security in their own ability on the journey – they have no need to "show off" or demonstrate their prowess unnecessarily. They know that the journey is not about them, but about those they are guiding.

Evolutionary Guides also *are masters of subtle course correction.* They have the ability to offer a constant stream of course-correcting adjustments that are subtle and never make people feel stupid, or humiliate anyone, or are designed to "show off" their own expertise. Evolutionary Guides have good judgment. They see more, they hear more, and they can make reasoned decisions. For this reason, Evolutionary Guides are rarely surprised. They are aware of the surrounding and dynamics of a journey and are not afraid to make decisions with lack of data or limited time. Judgment occurs routinely and consistently with obviously held and relevant values. This sort of quiet and reassuring confidence is the reflection of "being of" their environment.

Perhaps the most important characteristic of Evolutionary Guides is that they have no *predetermined definition of success* around the journey. They are open-minded about how a challenge can be met effectively, the paths available to success, and what a winning strategy might be. This is harder to do than it sounds. The balance between offering sound judgment and also remaining open to unexplored possibilities is a delicate one to master. Evolutionary Guides also make no predetermined judgment about which team members are going to take the lead on the journey. Just as on a trail hike unexpected leaders may emerge, the same will be true in your organization. Transformative change is inherently disruptive, and as your organization becomes less stable, moving through the change, new leaders – Evolutionary leaders – will rise to the surface.

They may not be the people you expect. They may not hold official leadership titles in the company. But they will be the ones you need. Evolutionary Guides are quick to recognize these people and make space for them to take the lead for the success of the journey.

So what does this mean for developing a high-performance Evolutionary Board? It means that the single most important role for the Board is to anticipate and plan for significant changes, both internal and external, that the organization will face. Think of it as "reading the rapids." The digital business environment is unforgiving if you are unable to operate at a very fast tempo. Evolutionary Boards do two things: they trust and empower their Senior Management to handle the day-to-day, month-to-month "paddling" through the rapids, and they are always working to get a better view of what's coming up. Ironically, we believe that the digital tempo of business demands a longer view of the future and we reject the idea that "because everything is changing so fast we can't make a plan." Evolutionary Boards have figured out how to bring powerful intelligence from other guides into the boardroom. They are quick to hike downstream themselves (by looking at other organizations, attending appropriate conferences, commissioning research, etc.) to see what the future holds. Their plans both react to their assessment of the future and most importantly take control of that future. They put the organization in a fundamentally proactive and offensive position. This difference is felt all through the organization. There are huge implications for efficiency, quality, recruitment and morale. When the people in an organization know that have a strong guiding body they can rely on, they are able to focus on the mission and are able to unfold their complete potential. If on a long hike you can trust that your guide is navigating well, you are free to concentrate on each step, optimizing your own performance and even helping those around you succeed.

We can't stress enough that Boards and Senior Teams frequently and dramatically underestimate their actual power and influence.

Just as we cannot not communicate, people in leadership positions cannot not lead. Evolutionary Guides know that everything they do is being understood as an act of guidance.

CHAPTER 8
Evolutionary Women

During the writing of this book we have been working with a large financial services client in the South that is pursuing an audacious 10-year strategic vision. Part of that 10-year transformation includes a succession plan for CEO that will place a woman in the executive seat for the first time in the company's history. Both the Board of Directors and the current CEO are supremely confident that she is the right person to shepherd the company into the future. But it is a big change for a workforce that has grown comfortable with the status quo. The current CEO reached out to us to produce a custom-designed development plan for her to prepare for the unique challenges of leading the organization through this inspiring change. While chatting with her candidly about the way the organization will adjust to a strong, confident and decisive female CEO, she expressed concerns over some employee comments that they did not have confidence in her abilities to lead well. She said, "I guess I just need to change my personality…"

We are willing to bet that without even meeting this amazing woman, you will agree that she absolutely DOES NOT need to change her personality! Sure, all of us have leadership competencies that we can develop further, areas of weakness that we can manage better, and new methods for soliciting feedback that we can master. And she is no different. The woman in this example is someone we have come to know well through our work together. And we can say without a doubt that she is an Evolutionary. Not a few weeks after this event, we were contacted by another female executive selected by her Board of Directors to accept the CEO position for her organization as the first woman in that role. She would like to go through a similar development program. We couldn't finish this book without exploring the question: "Why do highly competent executive women come to believe that they need to change who they are in order to achieve levels of top leadership?"

There is an old joke used frequently in Human Resources circles: "Mobile technology is the most disruptive thing to happen to the workplace since women entered it in the 1940s!" Since women entered the workforce, they have come a long way. Today girls outnumber boys in high school graduation rates, college enrollment, and school leadership positions. For the first time in United States history, in 2010 more women were employed in our country than men. And while some may say the progress has been too slow, women are now in line for CEO positions across the nation. Many of these women are Evolutionaries. They have had to be to get where they are – to break new ground in their industries and to be the "first" in these positions. These Evolutionaries have a lot to teach us about transformative change, courage and tenacity. And there are good financial reasons for organizations to pay attention to what they have to say.

Evolutionary Wisdom

CINDY TORTORICI: *Today, my business centers around helping women gain "A Seat at the Table" and I design workshops and events to coach women in these roles. After working for Saks Fifth Avenue and then later working eleven years for Nike, I took a ten-year sabbatical and for the first time I had time to reflect. I believe women become disadvantaged once they reach the senior ranks. Women do very well up through mid-management, racking up achievements through their ability to be tactical, multi-task, manage people, but when that early career success propels them into the senior positions, the game changes dramatically, and that is where women lack the* *resources they need to play the game well. Women know that they need to become more strategic and less tactical to succeed in these top positions, but they will still think differently than men do. First, this is not a bad thing. Second, women can think strategically in ways that men can't – seeing more facets, relationships and nuances associated with a problem and offering a different sort of creativity in solving those problems. But, often there is no one around to help them practice using these skills.*

Most of the women I talk to in senior executive positions feel lonely. There are very few women in the arena to begin with, so finding a mentor, a colleague, a coach, a friend can be difficult. And, unlike men in these posi-tions, there is no built-in culture because we are still too new to the game.

So, now we have our answer. Often the reason women feel, once promoted to C-suite positions, that they need a "personality trans-plant" in order to succeed is because there is no example around them of how to be a woman in these roles. But times continue to evolve, and Evolutionary women like Cindy Tortorici, Chandra Brown and the executives in our story are paving the way for those to come – transforming the role of CEO and their organizations in the process.

CHANDRA BROWN: *Being a woman at Oregon Iron Works has been a unique experience and it is different for a woman at the company than it would be for a male in a similar role. Oregon Iron Works has always been very supportive of me as I have moved forward in my role, but it has cer-tainly taken hard work. One of the things that I learned early in my career is that you need to be able to stand up and state what you want, what you don't want, and where you are going moving forward. I see a lot of women, especially younger women, take a passive role. You have to make your voice heard and sometimes that can be challenging for women as they move up the ranks. Making your voice heard means standing up if you don't believe in something, speaking out in board meetings, it means being the person who presents ideas, asking questions, setting up a meeting with someone if you want to know more details about something. People won't always be recep-tive to these behaviors, because they may not be used to seeing women in these roles – but that's what it takes to be a good executive, a good leader.*

The critical difference I see between men and women is that women don't stand up as often, they don't raise their hand or speak as loudly once they enter more male-dominated areas of business. I think it is because they feel they stand out more in a mostly male environment when they do raise their hand. As a woman in a male-dominated business when I walk into a room I usually stand out. I may be the only woman in the room or I may be the youngest person in the room but I think it is fantastic because when I make a point everyone will remember that point because of who delivered it. So you can look at it as a difficulty or as a negative but I look at it very much as strength. It can be a huge strategic advantage as you move forward.

*And I think to be successful as executives, women need to have a tool belt with a bunch of different tools in it. And this is something I think women can actually do better than men. Sometimes you need to use your "sweet and charming" tool and other times you need to use a tool for fine-tuning – maybe asking questions. I think of that as a small screwdriver. And yes, occasionally you need to pull out a big mallet and hammer something down. But what I see is that when that mallet is called for, most women find they do not have it in their tool belt. They just never acquired that tool. Different situations call for different tools, and there may be some tools you use really often and some you only use on rare occasions. My advice to all women is that you have **all** the tools and be skilled in using each one of them. Sometimes you back down and be charming and sometimes you confront things head on with the mallet and you stand up and call people out when they have clearly stepped out of line.*

Many times when women engage in aggressive behaviors such as those Chandra encourages, they are tagged with labels like "dragon lady," "domineering" or even just "mean." There is no question that Chandra is smart, driven, and ambitious. But ambition in a woman often carries negative connotations in our society. Chandra embraces her aggressive side as a strength – one aspect of what has helped her to be a successful and nationally respected leader in innovation and manufacturing today. But she is also quick to explain that although she rarely has to use her full aggressive strength in most business situations, the important point is that she knows she can and those she works with know it too. And, she admits, this sort of behavior will often incite strong reactions in others.

CHANDRA BROWN: *There is no doubt that there is a time in every woman's life or really every leader's life where you are going to receive backlash and there are a variety of different ways of handling that backlash. It comes down to direct communication. In my experience, it isn't useful to give the warm fuzzy approach when someone is really upset with you. It's better to ask exactly what the issue is, and then how to make it better. If someone is genuinely trying to be constructive in their intent, then I will engage with them and ask to take the conversation offline to see if we can find compromise. Other times though you are truly being challenged, and I think that's when it is the hardest for women. In those instances I think you need to meet the challenge where it lives – if someone is being obstructive or deliberately misleading others you have to stand up and say, "No, I totally disagree with you, and that's completely wrong. You are completely out of line." Use direct language and be clear. Of course every situation is unique, and it depends on the circumstances and the individual, but I do think sometimes when you are in a room with very powerful men and you don't like what they are saying or the way they are talking to you it's best to confront that behavior head on. That's not always the most successful way, it's not a 100% guaranteed option, but more often than not it has worked really well for me.*

Wow! If you are anything like us, you break into a cold sweat just thinking about the situation Chandra describes above. But the trick to being confident in such confrontations is to be sure you really know your stuff. When we speak from expertise, we feel more sure of ourselves. Evolutionary women push boundaries. And this inevitably means conflict will arise from time to time. The best way to navigate through debate, clash, and challenges is to have a reputation as a credible professional in your line of business and feel confident enough to take a stand in those occasions that require it. And for this reason, Evolutionary woman are constantly tending to their credibility.

CHANDRA BROWN: *Being able to make your points successfully comes from your own personal strength and credibility. You need to feel secure in what you are saying so you have to be well-versed and knowledgeable about whatever issue you are discussing. Whether you are a man or a woman, one of the greatest things that give people courage is being an expert on the topic in the room. If you are looking for the courage to speak up, my best advice is to make sure you really know what you are talking about. If I am going into a meeting on a topic, I will do the extra reading, do a little extra homework to make sure that I feel very comfortable with that topic and that shines through when I speak up. And confidence breeds confidence so if you speak up the first few times and you take those difficult steps, then it becomes easier with time. Not every idea or suggestion is going to be taken and sometimes there will be backlash for speaking up. But as you gain confidence it's not even an issue of courage anymore, it becomes easier to say, "I am voicing my opinion because I feel it is right, I have faith in it, I have confidence in it, and I would like it to be heard."*

Why You Need Evolutionary Women

In their book *Womenomics*, Claire Shipman and Katty Kay shocked the business world with a mountain of data proving that "putting women in charge is good for a company's bottom line." Studies conducted in nearly 200 of the Fortune 500 companies concluded that those organizations that were better at promoting women to senior positions experienced higher returns than those that did not. A series of studies documented in the book indicated that women executives in top management were better at promoting teamwork, motivating employees and fostering a creative environment. All of which are essential in fast-paced, innovative companies desiring transformative change. Evolutionary women are more willing to step into these roles, to be the "first" among their peers to hold these positions, and are most likely to put a "higher cause" at the center of their work over personal ambition and rewards.

And these benefits translate to placing Evolutionary women

on Boards of Directors as well. Research organizations Catalyst and McKinsey & Company have pioneered research linking gender balance and Board performance, showing that Boards with three or more women gained a significant performance edge over the competition, including 73% return on sales, 83% return on equity and 112% return on invested capital. Other aspects of the study show that when women have a strong representation on Senior Executive Teams those companies exceed peers in nine different performance criteria. This is not a book about data – but it's hard to ignore these and hundreds of other studies over the last five years that seem to continuously produce statistics that are nothing short of astonishing.

By now you are probably thinking, "OK, so if placing women at a senior level is so good for an organization's financial bottom line, why don't we see more women in these positions? Why isn't everyone promoting them?" Well, first, these women are tough. Evolutionary women are smart, no-nonsense, and quick to reject the business-as-usual cultural expectations that can arise from decades of "good-ol'-boy" management practices. Second, they are, for the most part, fed up with the status quo and looking for ways to work better, smarter, and with more integrity. They keep score differently. They measure success differently. In short, they are bound to shake things up a bit just by virtue of being different. It's not that there is a shortage of great talent in the pool – over 50% of middle level managers are women. So if you are still reading this, and your company is in need of transformational change and an increase in profitability, recruit a few Evolutionary women.

Evolutionary Women:
- *Are willing to be the first*
- *Establish credibility early and often*
- *Build a network of other Evolutionary Women*
- *Dream big*

One of the most courageous qualities that Evolutionary women possess is that they *are willing to be first*. Most of these women are pioneers in workplace domains long dominated by men – political office, corporate executive suites, boards of directors, medicine, technology, consulting, law and more. They are ready to cope with the loneliness they will feel as they spend most of their time with groups of men, and find that the occasional women they come across also view them as "set apart" because of the unconventional career choices that Evolutionary women tend to make.

Evolutionary women know that they are an exception to the norm when it comes to their position and behavior in the business environment. So, they accept that they will need to *establish their credibility early and often* in their careers. They will need to prove their credibility every time they meet someone new. That may not be fair, but it's a fact of life for them. They learn not to take it personally, and they just do it. They are resigned to the idea of proving themselves over and over again. They become very good at talking about what they do and why it matters. They know how to talk about ideas with enthusiasm and how to energize the people around them. They are not afraid to bring their passion and energy to the table, knowing that that combination of conviction and passion with the right data and evidence is the magic formula for bringing people along with them in their mission.

And they are authentic. They are constantly battling that voice in their heads that says, "For this job, you will have to change your personality." Too many women in business feel that they need to change themselves in order to fit in. Because Evolutionary women have come to peace with the idea of being more isolated than those around them, they are able to hold onto who they really are. This doesn't mean that Evolutionary women no longer care about relationships. Like any Evolutionary, they see relationships as paramount. But they accept that they may never be completely understood by the people they work with. They will have to find their support system somewhere else. Which leads us to our next point.

Evolutionary women know that they need to *build a network of other Evolutionary Women*. They quickly learn that the key to hanging onto who you are is to find people that are trying to do the same sorts of Evolutionary things in the world and build a connection with them. Cindy Tortorici tells us that once women get to a senior level they are expected to shift from being task-oriented superstars to visionary strategists. But they don't have the same access as men to networks where the rules of the game are explained as a matter of course. So Evolutionary women are pro-active – they seek out other women who have taken this journey before them (but are likely in another industry or organization) and ask them for their wisdom.

"We need someone who can tell us frankly that these are the rules, this is how they have changed from your last job, and this is how you need to work and communicate differently and this is what is expected," Tortorici advises.

This desire to connect to other Evolutionary women is not just driven by the need to hold onto self, it is the only way to truly accomplish the kind of goals that real Evolutionaries aspire to – changing the world. Influential people have influential networks. People don't get much done by themselves, no matter how smart and powerful they are. Evolutionary women know that they are going to need to build coalitions of other women with common goals in order to get things done. And this connects to the funda-mental Evolutionary concept that "it's not about you" – that there is a larger community that you are responsible to and for in your work and in your life.

Finally, Evolutionary women *dream big*. Few can offer a better example of dreaming big than Chandra Brown.

CHANDRA BROWN: *I started working for an international freight sales company with offices in over 60 countries around the world. They are head-quartered out of Australia and a fairly male-dominated company. Over time, I became ultimately one of two women on the sales staff. And I learned with* *that first major job that I could handle being in a work environment with primarily men. I enjoyed breaking some of the barriers for women in industry. I actually started at Oregon Iron Works as a temp and from a temp over 16 years I am now Vice President of Oregon Iron Works and President of the subsidiary United Streetcar. What I really like about Oregon Iron Works is its excellent leadership and that even though it is a bit of a rough and rugged more male work culture, I actually enjoy seeing things be built. Something that I realized early was that as a leader I want to touch what we build, I want to feel it, I want to walk on it. So, when we build a bridge I want to walk on that bridge. When we build a streetcar I want to ride on that streetcar; I want to be able to take my friends and my relatives on it. I like to lead people from a single idea to getting funding, through the building process and then see it function for the community. It is an incredible gift to be able to see something from its inception completely through to fruition and then be running for the next 30 years into the future.*

Chandra is the consummate Evolutionary. She thinks in the future, and is willing to navigate through a lot of disparity, unfairness, and doubt to see her transformational visions come to life. At heart, all Evolutionaries are dreamers. Thinking big is just a part of who they are. It's in their DNA.

In her book *The Curse of the Good Girl,* Rachel Simmons laments that girls in the United States are incredibly high performers, collecting "achievements by the handful" in school, but often don' t have the confidence to own them. She tells us that young women are consistently outpacing young men in academic programs, but continue to represent only a third of business school students and a quarter of law-firm partners. "If you look at girls on paper, they're terrific," says Simmons, but that performance is not translating into the leadership sphere as adults.

Evolutionary women are not born Evolutionary. They are a product of their own hard work, combined with talent sets, mentoring, opportunities, and an environment conducive to developing Evolutionary potential. The most future-thinking Evolutionary women are investing in the next generation, encouraging these high-achieving girls to chase their dreams.

Final Note: All of our Evolutionary characteristics in this book are consistent with the principles of androgyny that assume no person is beholden to a set of archetypical behavior that limits them. The androgynous person is successful in more situations because he or she doesn't have to adhere to a role that is solely masculine or feminine. It's not gender-neutral, but it is not gender-*constrained*. In other words, to be an Evolutionary is to be adaptable to the needs of a given transformative challenge, regardless of the masculine or feminine characterization of those necessary behaviors.

So, whether you believe that Evolutionary women are just "acting like men" or that they truly bring something unique and valuable to the game, the point is this:

1. We need to promote more women to leadership positions – if not because it is the *right* thing to do, then simply because it is the *profitable* thing to do.
2. Evolutionary women, especially those who have "made it," need support networks beyond what most current male-dominated leadership teams can provide. They should be encouraged and supported in these efforts.

CHAPTER 9

The Code of an Evolutionary

Realized Evolutionaries are rare. Many people have some of the qualities, but not all of them. We estimate that maybe five out of a thousand people are true Evolutionaries. That is one of the reasons why the Evolutionary code is so important. The self-aware Evolutionary has a huge amount of power, and that should mean that they also have a huge level of responsibility – a code of conduct that guides them.

The cornerstone of the code is a commitment to a cause that is larger than the individual. The pursuit of personal excellence is always in some fashion at the *service* of that larger cause. This larger cause is rooted in making the world a better place – leaving a positive and healthy legacy for generations to come. Evolutionaries understand that there is very little in this world of value that has not been created on the leveraged power of strong relationships between people. It takes teams to get most of the great work of the world done. We are interconnected, and those connections must be fundamentally understood and honored – and Evolutionaries know that this core relationship-building is the key to achieving truly great and lasting outcomes.

If you have read this book to this point and you find yourself resonating with the ideas that we have shared, and if you have found yourself nodding in agreement, or saying, "Finally, someone gets the way I feel!" then you may in fact be an Evolutionary. Chances are that you feel misunderstood by a lot of people. Chances are you resent it when people look at one of your actions and trivialize the reason for it. If you really want to upset an Evolutionary, question their motives. Because that is the whole point for an Evolutionary – *why* you are doing something is a very big deal!

The Evolutionary Code: We Know Why

This simple statement holds a lot of meaning. It means that you may be following, but you are not following blindly. You may be leading, but you are not driven by ego. You know why you are doing what you are doing and why it matters for a larger cause. You may find yourself with multiple layers of motives that are in play in a given situation or job, but there is an integrity at the foundation of all of those motives. A good example is the television show *M*A*S*H*, where the characters were faced with some very difficult choices, but the one constant was the reverence for preserving life and minimizing suffering. Though they were not always able to achieve those goals they always strived for them, even if it meant breaking some "rules" to stay oriented to those core values.

Evolutionaries may even feel like it is not worth the effort to do something unless several positive values are achieved at one time. Evolutionaries are looking for ways to create ecosystems of positive change that reinforce each other.

We Know Why means exercising your best judgment at any given moment. You cannot put a formula on how that judgment works, but if you make poor choices, you need to ask yourself how could you have judged better in that situation? What can you do to better inform your judgment as you evolve?

So what are the characteristics of Evolutionaries that follow the code?

Realized Evolutionaries are:
- *Deeply compassionate*
- *Transparent*
- *Courageous*

- *Trustworthy*
- *Committed to excellence as a form of SERVICE*
- *Legacy-minded*

You cannot be a true Evolutionary and not be **deeply compassionate.** Evolutionaries are not ashamed of the compassion they carry into every situation they encounter. We are not saying that all Evolutionaries are Mother Teresa (though she certainly was an Evolutionary), but all Evolutionaries do genuinely care about other people and about the future we leave for the next generation. Put simply, you cannot be aloof to suffering and be an Evolutionary.

Evolutionaries know that a **transparent** motive is the key for being an effective influencer. If the motive is pure and people can see that about you, you will naturally begin to garner followers. Transparent leadership is another hot buzz word in business today. As the impact of the Great Recession continues to resonate with people, trust in leadership is at an all-time low in our country. Transparency tends to be a term used to talk about sharing documents, conducting open meetings, and including as many people as possible in every decision. But all of these things are just a Band-Aid on a cancer – the real issue is that we don't trust the motives of the people running Wall Street, the people on Capitol Hill, and the people reporting our news. Real transparency is about laying your motive on the table, doing the right thing, and following through on your promises – something realized Evolutionaries do every day.

Evolutionaries live by a simple rule of thumb: If it's tough, it is probably the right thing to do. And doing the right thing is almost always a **courageous** act. Evolutionaries know that transformative experience is almost never about making things easy or simple, it is about fighting the dragons of complexity and not giving up – a sort of resolute approach, a willingness to take hits, to fail, to take risks, to offer personal sacrifice and abandon old rules in order to further the cause – even if that cause can't be fully accomplished in one's lifetime – which leads to our next point.

Evolutionaries are *trustworthy.* It's as simple as that. Evolutionaries are people that you would trust with your pocketbook and your children as well as your business. It's not that they are perfect. They might make a mistake, but they would tell you they made it, how they made it, and what they learned from it. Because they are comfortable with who they are, confident in their values, and unafraid of showing their "authentic selves" to the world, Evolutionaries are trusted individuals. Because they are compassionate and able to think beyond themselves and their own self-interests, people can believe in them. They keep their promises and they honor their commitments. You will often see Evolutionaries in long-term committed relationships. They view trust as a matter of honor.

In our company, we live and breathe the mantra that "there is no substitute for personal excellence." Evolutionaries are no strangers to the pursuit of greatness. They will strive for years to master competencies they believe are important. But unlike the individual that pursues excellence for the sake of excellence, Evolutionaries are *committed to excellence as a form of SERVICE.* Evolutionaries understand that the most important work of their lifetime will be realized in the context of fulfilled potential – their own and the potential of those that they teach, coach, and lead. Evolutionaries have no set level of expectations for what "success" is. Instead, by *realized potential*, we mean that Evolutionaries recognize that some people can give more than others, learn more than others, bear more weight than others, are simply capable of more than those around them. So they don't have preconceived notions of what it means to be excellent – the point is that the more you are capable of, the more you should do. Evolutionaries know they are capable of a great deal. And so they hold themselves to a higher standard.

But, while the Evolutionary may achieve great status in his or her career, the relationship to another person is never optimized from the consideration of being "one up" or "one down" in any regard. They are not keeping score. That does not mean an

Evolutionary won't tell you what to do or that an Evolutionary can't be told what to do, but it means that the score keeping is not a feature of the relationship. It's about being fiercely committed to excellence *and at the same* time not interested in who is better than whom. This is a rare blend. Many people are committed to excellence but also keep score. And many people don't keep score, but also don't aspire to achieve. Evolutionaries are able to achieve excellence while not keeping score, because competition with others is not what drives the Realized Evolutionary. The downside to this is that Evolutionaries may not always give recognition as well as they should, because they themselves are not in as much need of it.

Evolutionaries live in the future. They are **legacy-minded** in the way they approach their work and their life. They have both the ability to and desire to think in future-oriented terms. Evolutionaries care about the future, their participation in it and how they can best use their individual potential to make the world a better place through the work that they contribute in their lifetime. The Evolutionary has a responsibility to people younger and people older than them. They are conscious of the generational nature of life and are willing and able to adapt their messaging to each generation. Evolutionaries are acutely aware that we reap what we sow, and have a sensibility for making an investment – they know that as the generation before us did for us, we do now for them. Evolutionary people really do think several generations down the road. They think in terms of the legacy of an organization or community. They are very comfortable thinking outside of their own life span. They see the work they do almost as a part of a great relay race – this life is about running only one leg – what will you do with the baton in the very short time that you have it before you have to pass it on to the next teammate? To look generations backward and generations ahead is a point of maturity as an Evolutionary. You will recall from Chapter 1 of this book that there are degrees of Evolutionaries. It is only in the level of mastery that Evolutionaries truly understand the way in which their lifetime is just one very small part of the story that they are playing a role in. Only at the ultimate achievement – mastery – do we realize how small we actually are.

MAKING MAGIC: When people are obviously living by the Code of the Evolutionary, they are attracted to and attractive to others who are also living the code. So, by living the Code, you gain access to whole networks of Evolutionary people who are also trying to change the world for the better in core ways. And they are also willing to help each other, share ideas, explore opportunities, and invest in communities. These networks create the Evolutionary ecosystems that can facilitate the kind of good work that those around us often label as a "miracle" or "magic." People will often look at an event, new idea or altruistic community activism and say, "How did that happen?" It happens through the phenomenal informal networks of people who openly and proudly share a Code that drives innovation, good work and a beautiful future for generations to come.

CHAPTER 10

When Evolutionaries Fail

We have said before in this book that no one would want a whole organization full of Evolutionaries. This sort of lack of balance would mean details are missed, systems are underdeveloped, and procedures inconsistent, just to name a few problems. Because Evolutionaries are inherently collaborative, they often reveal plans or visions before they are fully baked and those plans are destroyed by the potentially well-meaning but nay-saying "realists" that surround them. Evolutionaries often do not realize that there is a lot of lonely work to be done before they can unveil their idea to others. The assumption that others will want to be a part of a ground-floor collaboration, and that they will want to work through the options and problem-solve an idea with you, is often a false one. In fact most people simply don't have the capacity, the patience, or the curiosity to spend time exploring something new, so they are hardwired to avoid change.

Evolutionaries can also fail because they are morally opposed to head games and politics – remember, they are the very definition of transparency. And that would work in an ideal world. But the reality of business is that to be successful, sometimes you have to play the political games, offer the favors, and make the questionable compromises. This is not to say that because people are not generally interested in new ideas, and politics often rules the day in any organization, that Evolutionaries would be better off to shut others out. This does not mean that Evolutionaries should abandon their commitment to collaborative dialogue and planning. But the Evolutionary will fail when he or she does not establish the right level of expectation when introducing a new idea. The simple way to say it is: the failed Evolutionary does not recognize the threatening quality of even the most positive suggestion.

Most of the time it is good that people avoid change. Even good change involves a risk; we are hardwired as a human race to avoid risk, so even good change is resisted. This sort of behavior is ingrained in us to preserve us – it's based in all sorts of survival instincts we've had since our race began. But Evolutionaries operate in what Kenneth Burke refers to as a "comic frame" – external inputs and outputs are part and parcel to what they are all about. The unexpected in this frame is just a part of the reality and is often welcomed. "Tragic-framed" people (or, most people) may have real trouble with an Evolutionary. This is a "closed loop" approach to life that constantly screens and rejects inputs that would disrupt the current worldview of the individual. Burke also makes the point that both of these frames are central to the human condition. It is not that one is good and one is bad. But what it does mean is that when an Evolutionary bumps up against a person who has a more dogmatic, black and white view of the universe, there will likely be tension. This tension is also not good or bad. Evolutionaries fail when they are not able to navigate and appreciate the conflict as generative. Instead, they become blocked and defined by the conflict, dismissing information or ideas that may be of value.

Evolutionaries attract followers for a variety of reasons, and those reasons are very important. Evolutionaries fail when they misunderstand or ignore the reasons for which people are following. For example, people may follow an Evolutionary out of sympathy rather than commitment to a cause that is bigger than the individuals involved. If you are sick – physically or emotionally – you will struggle with an Evolutionary dynamic because people will want to take care of you. That's not a bad thing – it can be good to show vulnerability and accept compassion. The realized Evolutionary will leverage the compassion of others to address something larger. If an Evolutionary has cancer, he or she will deflect conversations about his or her own way of dealing with the illness and instead will want to talk about how to eradicate cancer from the world. The way they ask for help is to solve something bigger. But Evolutionaries fail when they are unable to deflect tragedy (or a windfall) and allow it to get in the way of what they know to be the real focus of their life's work. This is not about being a "hero" or being "invincible" – it is at its core a fundamentally human response. It is a response driven by vision, commitment to excellence, the drive to leave a legacy and compassion rather than self-pity or self-obsession. The point is that we are defined as much by the people that follow us as by the vision we pursue. You don't need to look far to find examples of well-intended organizations that are brought down by followers who do not share the standards of integrity established by the leaders. Just as the motive for leadership is integral to successful leadership, the motive of the followers must be in alignment to achieve true Evolutionary change. It's not enough that the motives are clear to the Board, to leadership, or even to the public – the "Why" question that Cindy Tortorici explains is critical for leaders to know must also be answered by everyone in the organization.

Just as we want followers to follow the vision, and not the Evolutionary who created it, Evolutionaries fail when they lead from a place of ego rather than purpose. Just like anyone else, Evolutionaries fail when they drink too much of their own Kool-Aid – when they start to believe it is about them instead of about the work, the organization, the community. When this happens, you are no longer, by definition, an Evolutionary. As you read in the Code of an Evolutionary chapter, there is a need for clarity and diligence to keep the values front and center. It is OK to be personally invested in the transformative change that you are trying to accomplish (Evolutionaries always are) and it is normal to have moments where you temporarily lose sight of the real goal; the trick is to interrupt the delusional thought pattern that puts you in the center of the universe.

Evolutionaries also fail because they underestimate the power of a really good idea and a really good vision. When you look at communities that are achieving truly great things, you almost always wonder, "How did that start? How did that take hold?" One of the best examples of this is the "End Polio" campaign conducted by Rotary International. Twenty-five years ago Rotary, more to the point Rotarians – real people – set out with the audacious goal of eliminating the scourge of polio. Now, we are on the brink of completely eradicating the disease. This achievement went well beyond fundraising to embracing the entire cycle of behavior, medicine, prevention, education and governmental support that would be necessary to end polio. Rotary established a framework that offered a variety of "entry points" for key partners to engage in the effort. This super-powerful vision to change the world flourished precisely because Rotary invited people to participate in a solution and people stepped up. People are looking for these sorts of solutions. They are hungry for it. Scale is a part of what an Evolutionary is all about – making a difference in the world, for the community, for the universe – not just triple bottom lines, but triple *triple* bottom lines – Evolutionaries fail because they don't play on a big enough stage, often because they have been told one too many times that this sort of dream is impossible and they began to listen.

Evolutionaries can also fail because they suffer from the belief, "How hard can it be?" Evolutionaries are notoriously prone to underestimate the complexity of innovative ideas and be overly optimistic in the ability of their team to overcome obstacles. Because they readily see the maximum potential of those around them, they are prone to automatically assume people will naturally fulfill their potential when presented with a problem or a challenge. In fact, this is not the case. Most people never reach their potential. And for this reason, most people surprise Evolutionaries by not "rising to the task" and making the impossible happen. Evolutionaries are devastated by this reality, but never seem to learn from it. They move on eagerly and optimistically to the next new idea, new project, new team and miraculously have the same expectations that the people around them will rise to the occasion and fulfill their maximum potential and change the world together. The Evolutionary keeps believing, though, because every once in a while, people come through. Like a slot machine that pays off just enough to keep you standing there, Evolutionaries find just enough reward in seeing others rise to their highest potential that it confirms their optimism. So yes, Evolutionaries are a little crazy. To avoid failure, Evolutionaries should welcome the view of the pragmatist, the nay-sayer, the engineer, to keep them grounded and realistic about the capabilities of the talent they lead.

But the number one big reason Evolutionaries fail is because they don't have the discipline and attention span to pick up their good ideas and bring them to fruition. So when their idea is shot down by the team, they are often not ready or able to carry out their idea on their own. They need others to help them make their ideas real, so they need to be able to sell their ideas. This means that Evolutionaries need to get better at baking their ideas more completely before presenting them. And, when you inevitably present your next half-baked idea, and it gets shot down by the realists in the room, see that feedback as a blessing. It shows you the objection you need to prepare for in the next dialogue you pursue.

Finally, beyond the organizational weaknesses that most Evolutionaries possess, there is a genuine Dark Side to the Evolutionary personality. Often Evolutionaries fail because they are too open with their hearts, investing in the potential they see in others, dreaming big, and placing their own reputations on the line. By opening their hearts and minds so widely, by not deflecting or finding unhealthy ways of processing or coping with the intense lives they lead, they often invite deeper pain and heartache than most people can suffer. It is hard to care so much – about so much. Possessing the maturity to deal with (and carry) as much as they do is still an incredible burden. Being a Realized Evolutionary means walking an exhausting and heartbreaking path. But the payoff can be big too – the knowledge that you truly did your best in this life, gave all you had to give, and left the world just a little bit better place for having lived in it for a brief while.

The Evolutionary existence is based on gaining momentum through the accumulation of experience in service and transformation. It is about starting small, but thinking big. If after the previous paragraph you find yourself second-guessing the desirability of the Evolutionary lifestyle, that's OK! What you can do is recognize and support the efforts of the Evolutionaries around you who are driven to walk this path. As you conclude reading this book, you could choose to walk away with a broad, general impression of the potential of being an Evolutionary. Or, you could begin right now identifying specific concepts that inform challenges you are facing right now. You could identify specific questions that came out of your reading that you will take steps to answer. You could begin making incremental changes in your approach to conversations, planning, innovation, leadership and guidance. Or you could simply support the people who do with kind words, small gestures and whatever encouragement you can offer. These simple acts of support are critical for an Evolutionary to achieve transformative change.

Conclusion

We think an easy and powerful next step is to have a conversation with someone else who read this book. We think you will be amazed at how different another person's impression of the value and challenge of being or working with an Evolutionary can be. It is especially interesting to hear the point of view of an Evolutionary who has read the book. Our hope in writing this book is that we have created an invitation for people to talk about a worldview that has been hidden in plain sight for generations. For a true Evolutionary the recognition that you are not alone should be liberating and extremely compelling. For those who work and live with Evolutionaries it should be confirming of the opportunities and challenges you face in collaborating with, supporting and loving these rare people.

During the writing of this book we introduced the Evolutionaries term to many of the people we work with. And we are delighted when our clients talk to us about the Evolutionaries in their organizations. They are beginning to see the world differently. As this terminology takes hold, we see our clients developing a whole new view of what is possible, even though they are working with the same staff, the same resources, the same constraints and the same vision. The ability to name it and talk about it gives you the power to do what you could not do before. Language precedes and informs our perception of reality. The language of the Evolutionary experience is in itself transformative – allowing those who speak it to take control.

One more thing about Evolutionaries: they know when to stop pondering and start doing. The book is over. Time to get busy!

About the Authors

Randy Harrington, PhD is CEO and owner of Extreme Arts & Sciences and the co-founder and owner of Strategic Arts and Sciences and Best Practices Media. After completing his doctorate in organizational communication from the University of Oregon in 1992, he began his consulting career. With 20 years of experience, Dr. Harrington is now one of the premier consultants to financial institutions in the USA. He is a sought after strategic planner and executive coach as well as for his work in organizational change management and media messaging. His theories on the effectiveness of high-impact teams and communication push clients like Microsoft, Bluetooth SIG Inc. and the United Nations to work smarter and more efficiently. Dr. Harrington also earns lots of frequent flier miles—delivering keynote speeches each year to audiences from New York to Kyoto. He is an avid guitarist, cook, and scuba diver. He makes his home in Eugene, Oregon with his wife, Patty.

Carmen E. Voillequé is the CEO and owner of Best Practices Media, co-founder of Strategic Arts and Sciences, and Principal consultant for Extreme Arts & Sciences. She has over 15 years of experience in public speaking and facilitation and is nationally respected for her ability to provide advanced strategic planning for complex partnerships, systems, associations and networks to achieve significant organizational change. Ms. Voilleque has narrowed her focus to strategic planning and the development of high performance teams in the last five years of her career. She serves clients in finance, law, government, non-profit, technology, education, health care and hospitality. Her varied experience allows her to bring a combination of fresh perspectives and deep knowledge to her work with private, non-profit, and public organizations. Ms. Voilleque also logs her fair share of frequent flier miles to deliver keynote speeches across the nation. When not working, she enjoys traveling with her husband and daughter. She and her family make their home in Portland, Oregon.

To experience more Evolutionary stories, visit us at **www. Be-Evolutionary.com.**